# Killing Thinking: The Death of the Universities

Related title

*Where Have All the Intellectuals Gone?* – Frank Furedi

# Killing Thinking: The Death of the Universities

MARY EVANS

continuum
LONDON • NEW YORK

**Continuum**

The Tower Building
11 York Road
London SE1 7NX

15 East 26th Street
New York
NY 10010

*www.continuumbooks.com*

**British Library Cataloguing-in-Publication Data**
A catalogue record for this book is available from
the British Library.

ISBN  0–8264–7312–1 (hardback)
　　　0–8264–7313–X (paperback)

**Library of Congress Cataloging-in-Publication Data**
A catalogue record for this book is available from the Library of Congress.

Typeset by BookEns Ltd, Royston, Herts.
Printed and Bound in Great Britain by Cromwell Press, Trowbridge, Wiltshire

# Contents

# *Acknowledgements*

This book was written in troubled times, both personal and professional. During these months I was extremely fortunate to receive help and support from a number of people, all of whom provided care, concern and extraordinary kindness. My thanks, therefore, to John Baldock, David Boothroyd, John and Jean Buss, Sarah Carter, Rosemary Crompton, Hugh and Diane Cunningham, Kathy Davis, Richard de Friend, Martha and James Davis, Rod Edmond, Barbara Einhorn, Frank Furedi, Sarah Harman, Jill Hemmings, John Jervis, Terry Lovell, Pat Macpherson, Tracey Milliner, Anne Phillips, Steve Pollock, Lizzie Pollock, Karen Phillips, Frank and Kathy Parkin, Kate Reed, Miri Song, Howard and Deborah Stoate, Anne Seller, Janet Sayers, Jackie Stacey, Geoffrey Stephenson, Sarah Tong, Jenny Williams, Judith Webster, Steve and Jenny Uglow, Clare Ungerson and Akane Hubuki-Bedford.

Two final debts are considerable: first my thanks to Gemma Chapman for her skilled and patient typing. Second, thank you to David, Tom and Jamie for being there.

# *Introduction*

'The more it costs, the less it's worth'
(Student slogan, London, 2003)

This book was inspired by the experience of working in a British university in the latter part of the twentieth century and the first years of the twenty-first. It has not been a happy time, since those years have seen the transformation of teaching in universities into the painting-by-numbers exercise of the hand-out culture and of much research into an atavistic battle for funds. Academic life has become subject to a degree of bureaucratic control which needs urgent anthropological investigation as a new form of social life and universities would repay the investigation of trained ethnographers. The rich mix of species would be rewarding in itself, as would the contest between the spirit of the university past with the reality of the university present.

We are told that this world represents our best national hope for intellectual vitality and creativity. We are also told that we should pay more to enter it and to experience its rich resources. Yet those rich resources are increasingly marginalized by cultures of assessment and regulation, the heavy costs of which (both financial and intellectual) are to be carried by students. Increasingly, students are being asked to pay for the costs of the regulation of higher education rather than education itself. Hence the slogan which is quoted above. Access to higher education has become more widely available: the implications of that change are the concern of the following pages.

# Through the Looking Glass: or what Pierre Bourdieu and Kingsley Amis have in common

In the autumn of every year, thousands of students begin, or return to, degree courses at British universities. They are met by the standard form of welcome, which all institutions offer to initiates: registration, local information and a brief introduction to forms of possible discipline. Students are, of course, not deprived of their own clothes or subject to mandatory physical examination but they are expected to attend the welcome addresses of the major authority figures of the university. Most of those figures will be men, and so at the point in their lives when students leave their re-constituted and re-constructed modern families they are confronted with a world in which patriarchy is alive and well. But this book is not about patriarchy in the universities (although references to that point may occasionally emerge). Rather it is concerned with the content of contemporary British universities: the world inside what used to be described as the 'ivory tower' or, even more fancifully, the 'groves of academe'.

The words 'ivory' and 'groves' conjure up pictures of things that are rare and beautiful; a grove suggests pastoral scenes, contemplation in quiet places and a world of created beauty, while ivory invokes pictures of tiny, rare objects. Jane Austen, for example, once commented that her novels were fashioned out of a tiny piece of ivory. The words 'rare' and 'beautiful' are not, perhaps, the most likely words that many people would use to describe contemporary universities. Since the British government of Tony Blair made a determined commitment to educate half of every cohort of eighteen-year-olds in higher education (a figure not dissimilar from that of other Western countries), universities have become over-crowded places, physically ill-prepared for the numbers of students arriving on their doorsteps. The academics in these institutions have little or no time for contemplation, pastoral or otherwise, since our time is taken up with the new tasks of the university in an age of mass production. Finding an ivory tower in this world would be a major achievement; achieving entry to it a feat comparable to climbing Everest without oxygen.

At this point it would be possible to embark on a lengthy hymn to the departed university, a world of intellectual conversation, engaged students and limitless indulgence. To do so, as anybody who has worked in a university for any significant period would know, is to depart to the realms of fantasy. Universities in this country (and elsewhere) once admitted fewer students and were more or less entirely un-policed by the kind of bureaucratic Rottweilers now snapping at all our heels, but they were not necessarily admirable institutions. We have to establish, therefore, that we cannot easily defend the past, or invoke that past as an attack on the present. But what can be done, and it is the argument here, is to suggest that what universities have become is a distortion of the values of the academy. The shift suggested here is not, therefore, a shift from the very good to the very bad. Rather it is a shift from a collective world in which independent and critical thought was valued, to a collective world in which universities are expected to fulfil not these values but those of the marketplace and the economy. This discussion is not derived from a nostalgia for the past, but a fear for the future. In particular the concern which inspires these pages is that of the evolution of the universities into institutions which only serve a very small-minded master: the rational bureaucratic state of the twenty-first century.

This state, the child of the ill-matched parents of Enlightenment rationality and the market economy, has become (like many children of unhappily married parents) both unstable and fearful. Unstable in the sense that it lurches from crisis to crisis and fearful in the sense that it cannot endure a discussion of any idea or possibility outside its own experience. Often promiscuous in its behaviour and its allegiances, this state is nevertheless profoundly conservative in its choices and its values. Unfortunately for the social world, unhappy children do not always contain their unhappiness in their own domestic space. This particular unhappy child has now come to dominate the world in which we – and universities – live. In common with other unhappy children the needy state of the twenty-first century clamours for attention and recognition and its bottomless claims for endorsement are voiced by people such as Charles Clarke, the British Secretary of State for Education who, in 2003, voiced the view that education for its own sake 'was a bit dodgy'. This idea (widely attacked as it was) nevertheless made transparent the idea that education had no justification in its own terms. The implication of the remark was that values and priorities other than those of education should occupy a central place in universities; the comment made explicit the assumption that universities are expected to be instruments of the interest of the State.

Most of those people who have an interest in universities and higher education know that until the 1960s university education was an experience of few British people. The population as a whole did not go to university, nor was the expectation of higher education (in the sense of education after the age of eighteen) an established part of the cultural landscape of about half the population. (In 1960, there were eighteen universities in England; by 1966 this number had almost doubled.) When people went to university, prior to the British post-Robbins expansion of the

1960s, they went to a number of 'red-brick' universities or the universities of London, Oxford and Cambridge. The most famous satire of university life which has been published in Britain, Kingsley Amis's *Lucky Jim*, was set in one of those red-brick universities in which there was little that was either socially or intellectually distinguished. Indeed, what Amis captured in his novel was a dynamic of class relations in English universities: the intelligent lower-middle-class man (Lucky Jim) attempting to negotiate a world in which the upper class define their right to rule through cultural symbols. Jim Dixon's drunken attack on those symbols (the nostalgia for the past and the denigration of mass, and mass produced, culture) is a complex, but forceful argument about higher education and culture which repays considerable re-reading.

Published in 1954, *Lucky Jim* set out an account of class relations in higher education which is still relevant; the ex-President of the United States, Bill Clinton, once famously remarked, 'It's the economy, stupid', in reply to a question about political priorities. Amis recognized not the economy of higher education, but its culture and the centrality of ideas about culture, to ideas about education. In particular, Amis recognized both the part that universities play in bestowing cultural authority at the same time as they provide a location for genuinely creative work. Amis attacked the misuse of universities by a social élite; almost fifty years after the publication of *Lucky Jim* the misuse of the universities is more likely to be through authoritarian ideas rather than the authoritarian individuals who dogged the life of Amis's anti-hero Jim Dixon.

When Amis allows Jim Dixon to voice his feeling about universities he gives Dixon the space to voice two themes, both of which are relevant to contemporary universities. First, he allows Dixon to vent his spleen against the ways in which academics work. Here is Dixon assessing his own academic essay:

> Dixon had read, or began to read, dozens like it, but his own seemed worse than most in its air of being convinced of its own usefulness and significance. 'In considering this strangely neglected topic', it began. This what neglected topic? This strangely what topic? This strangely neglected what? His thinking all this without having defiled and set fire to the typescript only made him appear to himself as more of a hypocrite and fool.[1]

But what Amis does with this idea is more than to lampoon academic work. He also suggests that what Jim Dixon is actually doing might be useful; the problem is the format and the regulated organization of academic work, so that important issues can be buried or distorted by the processes and the structures within which they are produced. Dixon *has* to publish and therefore *has* to write articles in order to secure his career; it is these imperatives, rather than the activity itself, which produces works of mangled and ridiculous prose.

The comments quoted above are made by Jim Dixon at a moment of entire sobriety. In moments of extreme drunkenness Dixon does not become more tolerant of the academy but his sober self-loathing turns to anger against authority, whether personal (in the shape of his Professor) or general (the cultural dominance of what Dixon describes as 'the home-made pottery crowd, the organic husbandry crowd, the recorder-playing crowd').[2] Barely able to stand, Dixon delivers a public lecture which concludes with an attack on all those values and habits which he had most loathed in the university. Those pastimes which Dixon listed were not merely loathsome in themselves but loathsome because they were taken as marks of cultural superiority and a consequent right to assume authority over others. Jim Dixon's attack on 'Merrie Englande' is the beginning of those culture wars of post-1945 Britain, wars in which the democratization of culture and consumption that occurred after 1945 was fiercely contested. Access to universities was part of this contest. Jim Dixon makes no secret of the fact that universities are not part of his social world. But it is part of the argument of this book that the *apparent* democratization of the universities (certainly in terms of access) has done little to contribute to shifts towards a greater degree of democracy. The two words, although connected, are not necessarily socially related.

The figure against whom Jim Dixon directs his loathing and dislike is the Head of his Department, one Professor Welch. The name is appropriate, for

Welch is a man with a genius for avoiding work and delegating to others. Welch may appear as a fool, a man unable to negotiate a revolving door let alone more sophisticated forms of technology, but he matches Jaroslav Hasek's famous character Svejk in his ability to keep his distance from any form of effort. Initially a figure of fun and loathing to Dixon, Welch is finally presented as benign and we, as readers, might see Welch himself as a symbol of resistance to ideas about efficiency, hard work and application. Welch was not managerial material, except in the sense that he represented the class from which British managers (and Professors) were often drawn. What Welch represents is a set of upper-class expectations about a right to rule others, and to do so through the assertion of cultural superiority.

So the incompetence of the officer class is part of the theme of Amis's novel. To write a novel about the universities in order to make this point seems, at first sight, to be somewhat fanciful. Yet Amis, himself a university lecturer, and part of a generation of men who had served in the British Army and thus experienced the best, and the worst, of British Officers, clearly recognized the centrality of education to the post-war world. At the time of the publication of *Lucky Jim* university education was the preserve of a small minority of the population, but the popular culture of the time was increasingly recognizing the part that skills and abilities which were not confined to the upper-middle class were to play in a social world which was becoming increasingly self-conscious about being 'modern' and 'scientific'. Science-for-civilians (in the shape of cars, domestic machinery and other consumer goods) was in the process of transforming the domestic expectations of the British. This new world may have been what Richard Hoggart was famously to describe as a 'Candy Floss World' but it was one which was deeply attractive (and available) to millions of citizens.[3]

The comment cited by Hoggart above is in many ways deeply ironic. Hoggart was protesting (in 1957, the date of the first publication of *The Uses of Literacy*) against what he saw as the commercial exploitation of various forms of social life by the United States and the subsequent erosion of more organic forms of culture. The irony is that Hoggart, a man of the political left, should in retrospective appear to be defending precisely the kind of cultural conservatism that Amis – a man who moved from the political left to the political right – is attacking. Amis is now associated with the values of conservatism and reaction and *Lucky Jim* is consequently considered as part of the career of a man who was to criticize the expansion of the universities. But various arguments need to be disentangled here: arguments about class and cultural authority, for example, need to be separated from arguments about what would now be described as 'dumbing down'. We can read *Lucky Jim* as a hymn to democracy, scepticism and, most important of all, the rejection of cultural authority derived from class position. The university at which Jim

Dixon works (created from Amis's own experience as a Lecturer at Swansea University and a visit to Leicester University to see his friend, and dedicatee, Philip Larkin) is not in itself a comic institution. What becomes comic about it – and what incites Jim Dixon to drunken fury – is the assumption that education, and higher education in particular, is synonymous with the acceptance of certain cultural values, and values derived from the class position and experience of the educated upper-middle class. Thus the veneration of Welch and his wife for mediaeval England is implicitly about the veneration of a hierarchical, indeed feudal society, a society in which 'culture' was about the production of particular goods and the practise of certain cultural activities in ways which were socially exclusive. In what appears to be the innocent, if agonizing, exercise of playing folk music and reading Continental literature, lurks the expectation that these practices confer on the practitioner both separation from the majority, and equally important, authority over it.

*Lucky Jim* can, therefore, be read as a radical, and still disturbing critique of class-based expectations of cultural privilege and authority. The French social theorist Pierre Bourdieu has theorized precisely the same territory as Amis, arguing, in an essay in *Practical Reason*, that 'symbolic capital' (which includes culture) has a real value in the securing (and maintaining) of social position and privilege. He writes:

> Symbolic capital is any property (any form of capital whether physical, economic, cultural or social) when it is perceived by social agents endowed with categories of perception which cause them to know it and to recognize it, to give it value ...[4]

Alternatively, as Jim Dixon, speaking of Professor Welch, says:

> He wants to test my reactions to culture, see whether I'm a fit person to teach in a University, see? Nobody who can't tell a flute from a recorder can be worth hearing on the price of bloody cows under Edward the Third.[5]

Bourdieu and Amis both know how much culture, in all its forms, matters. In different ways each man lived through the re-writing and the re-positioning of culture in the 1960s and the 1970s: Amis came to express grave reservations about wider access to higher education, Bourdieu to argue against the seizing of 'high' culture for social privilege. But what the two men never abandoned was recognition of the relationship between class and culture: there was, to each of them, no sense in which a culture was ever 'class free'. The importance of this debate, and these ideas, to education, and particularly higher education, was equally apparent to both and it is thus that their ideas provide such a rich source for the discussion of what has happened – and is happening – to universities. We can see, in the work of these two men, a discussion of the themes that should, but all too often do not, inform debates about higher education. Among those themes are three which merit particular attention: the reason for universities; the relationship between universities, class and culture; and the appropriate form of organizing universities.

The first issue, that of debates about the rationale for universities, is one that has changed dramatically in the past fifty years. When Amis wrote *Lucky Jim* universities were still largely regarded as necessary training grounds for the social élite and the locus of essential scientific research. The nation needed literate diplomats, civil servants and all kinds of professional men who could be relied upon to recognize their own and the state's interests. At the same time the nation also needed scientific expertise of various kinds, and universities could (and did) provide this. Universities of this era were the preserve of white, middle-class men, in some ways part of Christopher Caudwell's 'dying culture' and the seedbed of the idiot, aggressive, military culture attacked by Virginia Woolf in *Three Guineas*.[6] But by the end of the 1950s a consensus had established the apparently uncontestable view that a highly educated – by which was meant educated at a university – population was necessary to maintain the economic and administrative functions of an advanced industrial society. The universities therefore acquired a new, and more central, part in debates about the prosperity of the nation. Furthermore, most Western social democracies came to see access to universities in the years after the end of the Second World War as both an individual right and a sensitive indication of the extent of social justice in a particular society.

These two principles, of social justice and economic necessity, were recognized by the British Robbins Committee which, reported in 1963, and stated that, 'courses of higher education should be available for all those who are qualified by ability and attainment to pursue them and who wish to do so'.[7] But the Robbins Report, although always taken as the transforming point in the history of twentieth-century British higher education, came at the end of a decade of expansion: the number of students in full-time higher education practically doubled from 122,000 in 1955 to 216,000 in 1962.[8] Thus while Robbins emphasized the continued need for expansion in higher education it was essentially about further expansions rather than the invention of an entirely new approach. The Robbins Report, in making recommendations about the necessary increase in numbers of students in higher education, further recognized the existing diversity of British higher education, from ancient to red-brick universities and from teacher training colleges to polytechnics providing clearly identified vocational training.

Higher education at the historical point just before its greater expansion was not, therefore, a homogeneous or nationally controlled exercise. What emerged as the ethos of post-Robbins', 'new' universities of the 1960s was an amalgam of liberal expectations and aspirations about education with more mundane hopes about the contribution of the 'new' higher education to the hoped for 'technological revolution' of the 1960s. The new British universities offered a broad-based curriculum, based on ideas about multi-, cross- and inter-disciplines. A new person was expected to emerge from a curriculum which reached (in the infamous description of a course at the University of Sussex) from 'Plato to Nato' and who embraced both the natural sciences and the humanities (most famously at the University of Keele). 'New' universities became rapidly popular with students, and the site of a set of cultural expectations about the meaning and the function of higher education.

Optimism was not, however, the only god-parent of the new universities. As soon as the construction of these new universities was agreed, voices were raised about, first, the kind of student about to be educated through post-Robbins expansion and, second, the nature (and indeed the quality) of the education that students would receive. When the University Grants Committee reviewed plans for the new University of York it commented that:

> The York Board claims that for undergraduates of the present age often lacking in family background conducive to students' habits and cultural interests pursued in common, residence is a part of the benefits of the University education whose value can scarcely be over-stressed.[9]

Or to put it another way, when that comment was made in 1962, university administrators had some concern about how, if at all, they were going to make silk purses out of the sow's ears about to descend upon them. In retrospect the uncontested cultural baggage contained in the remark is striking; public schoolboys at Oxbridge are unproblematic as undergraduates, but new arrivals from other destinations are going to need compensatory socialization to render them acceptable to the world of the universities.

The question of how to integrate students into the world of the universities takes us to the issue which was to challenge, and continue to challenge, universities throughout the 1960s and the 1970s, that of culture, and its particular manifestations in class, race and gender. It would be foolish to assume that class was not an issue for universities (and students and staff in them) in the Britain of the first fifty years of the twentieth century. Numerous writers have expressed their negative feelings about the 'Brideshead Revisited' aspects of Oxford and Cambridge: the domination of the public schools, the almost complete absence of women and ethnic minorities, the often erratic standards and the social exclusion of anyone not from the British ruling class. But at the same time British universities in these years were the home of Keynes, Rutherford, Hodgkin, Wittgenstein, J. H. Plumb and so on and on – to Anthony Bunt, Burgess and Maclean. Diversity was far from absent, even if expectations of homogeneity were the norm. It was this expectation of homogeneity which was to be shattered by what can only be described as the 'culture wars' of the 1960s and the 1970s, wars that also took place in the United States and much of Western Europe.

The 'culture wars' in the universities arose in part from global re-alignments in the relationships between generations. 'Youth' started to write what was originally his own script, but soon a script that was also being re-written for women. The sexual revolution of the 1960s and the massive political movements in the United States about Civil Rights and opposition to the war in Vietnam gave a new meaning to 'political' and the implications of that idea underpinned the numerous debates which began about questions of conventional authority and legitimacy. Students started to question what they were taught, and how they were taught it. Academics, seldom anxious to voice their protests through 'sitting in' at the very institutions where they were employed, also began to re-think the content and the nature of the curriculum. Two particular examples of the 'war' over the curriculum were the debate in the University of Cambridge English Faculty in the 1970s (a debate which became front page news and resulted in both staff resignations and some re-writing of the syllabus) and the many battles in universities in the United States over the absence of both women and ethnic minorities from social science and literature syllabuses.[10] The 'counter-culture' as it became known in the 1960s and 1970s was then blamed for all forms of cultural decline. Philip Larkin, in his youth the grammar school boy appalled by the amateurism of much of the teaching at the University of Oxford (and the author of a novel, *Jill*, about the bleak experiences and social misery of a grammar school boy at Oxford) came to pen the following lines:

> When the Russian tanks roll westward, what defence for you and me?
> Colonel Sloman's Essex Rifles? The Light Horse of L.S.E?[11]

The term 'culture wars', and much of the language used in the debates about it, suggests actual war: blood on the carpet of the Senior Common Room and fierce loathings. But, as Terry Eagleton has pointed out,

> The Clash between Culture and culture, however, is no longer simply a battle of definitions, but a global conflict. It is a matter of actual politics, not just academic ones ... it is part of the shape of the world politics of the new millennium. Though culture, as we shall see, is still not politically sovereign, it is intensely sovereign, it is intensely relevant to a world in which the joint wealth of the three richest individuals is equal to the combined wealth of 600 million of the poorest. It is just that the culture wars which matter concern such questions as ethnic cleansing, not the relative merits of Racine and soap opera.[12]

This passage was written in 2000, and its last sentence indicates an important shift on the part of an academic who once played an important role in those 'culture wars' which debated the content of the university curriculum. As Eagleton points out, the battle over 'culture' in higher education is no longer about what is taught, since by 2000 most Western universities had become pluralist in their definitions of appropriate curriculum in higher education. But what this indicates is a turning away from the previous liberal idea that people could become 'better' or 'educated' through the study of certain authors or ideas to the view that there is no necessary moral gain in the study of particular individuals or texts. This leaves universities with a moral vacuum at the heart of their teaching of the humanities, and to a certain extent the social sciences. (That sentence also raises the question, which needs more extensive discussion, of the way in which it is the humanities and the social sciences which have 'carried' the values of the universities. Battles about science in the universities have largely been about the sources of funding for science and seldom, particularly in a general sense, about the nature of the curriculum.)

The lost moral purpose of the teaching of subjects in the arts and social sciences is for many people an excellent and to-be-welcomed development. Not everyone endorses the idea that *Mansfield Park* and *Middlemarch* can teach us morality and thirty years of structuralism and feminism have taught us all deep scepticism about words such as the 'family' or 'deviance'. The liberal university of the 1960s and the 1970s, which widened its curriculum and extended its intake, nevertheless maintained the idea that higher education was about teaching, and about teaching a set of values and a certain familiarity with the process of critical inquiry. That model has, in Britain, largely been superseded by a new model which makes much more explicit the economic role of the universities. It is thus that universities become part less of 'culture' in the liberal sense of engagement with certain forms and kinds of knowledge but rather with a political culture which is manifestly about the furtherance of the aims of the Western state. To return to Eagleton's quotation: the 'culture war' over Racine or soap opera is long gone; the real culture war is about national politics and – if we extend the argument globally – about the legitimacy of Western assumptions.

In the twenty-first century we can suggest that a concern for Racine (or other aspects of 'high' culture) is possibly the new radicalism, as indeed is any interest in any work or set of ideas which is removed from the assimilative grasp of global capitalism. In making this suggestion what is voiced is a complete shift from the late 1960s and early 1970s when re-writing the curriculum to include mass culture and the culture of those 'minorities' such as women and non-white people was a radical activity. Courses about women, about post-colonial literature, about the British soap opera *Eastenders* and Madonna were not always welcomed with open arms; indeed they were more likely to provoke, on both sides, raised voices and clenched fists. But this new content did claim its place, and by the 1980s the study of 'mass' or 'popular' culture was a well-established part of the university curriculum. Protest about subject matter is not over, as recent criticisms of the so-called 'Micky Mouse' degrees of Media and Cultural Studies have demonstrated, but fierce opposition to the very idea of a more inclusive curriculum has disappeared. Mockery of degrees which include the study of footballers or garage music has become muted, not least because it has become apparent that a broader curriculum, and a broader intake to the universities, has done very little to shift either the nature of the British class structure as a whole or the location of significant academic power and resources. Indeed, the continuing dominance by the universities of Oxford, Cambridge and London of almost every evaluatory list in English higher education is an object lesson in the folly of under-estimating the intelligence of 'good ole boys'. Those 'old-type *natural* fouled-up guys' as Philip Larkin described himself, and his generation of Oxbridge educated men, might possess little in the way of experience of street culture, but they could transparently match its vigour and assertiveness.[13] As 'street fighting men' the Vice Chancellors of Oxford, Cambridge and London clearly took no prisoners.

The world in which Vice Chancellors of rich and privileged universities had to exercise themselves to maintain their privileges was one in which new forms of organization and assessment demanded all available skills of ingenuity and intelligence. If we wish to name a date on which these changes were introduced into English (and indeed British) universities then we have a number of dates from which we can choose. Marilyn Strathern has suggested that 1792 is a crucial date for universities, since it was in 1792 that a member of the University of Cambridge proposed that all answers in the tripos examination should be written as well as verbal. As Strathern comments:

> With measurement came a new morality of attainment. If human performance could be measured, then targets could be set and aimed for. What is became explicitly joined with what ought to be. This new morality was epitomized in the concept of improvement. 'Improvement' is wonderfully open-ended, for it at once describes effort and results. And it invites one to make both ever more effective – a process from which the tests themselves are not immune: measuring the improvement leads to improving the measures.[14]

It is perhaps cheering to be reminded that a culture of assessment and improvement is not the invention of the late twentieth century but the late eighteenth; equally academics may be depressed to see how little we have been able to intervene in what could be interpreted as a forced march toward systematic and intrusive audit.

The expectations about audit which now dominate universities do not, of course, simply extend, as they did in 1792, to the audit of students. Staff, both academic and non-academic have been included in the processes of audit, as have the many forms of regulation and assessment which universities now possess. In this world, a world which we can see as linked to 1792 by a history of post-enlightenment expectations of change, progress and nationality, the participants are offered what is presented as a democratic right. But just as apparent democracy becomes part of the apparent legitimacy of universities, so the definition of that experience becomes less democratic by virtue of the naming and the identification of the reasons for universities. In 1792 universities were not asked by the State to define their purpose, nor did the State think it part of its responsibilities to do so. In Britain this has now changed and less distant dates than 1792 mark shifts of considerable importance for universities. Two dates, in particular, stand out: the Jarrett Report of 1985 and the Dearing Report of 1997.[15] The Dearing Report of higher education explicitly stated that universities had four functions: they should 'be a significant force in the regional economy, support research and consultancy and attract inward investment, provide new employment and meet labour market needs and foster entrepreneurship among students and staff'.[16] This blue-print for the function and the behaviour of the universities met little open and explicit challenge from the most powerful in British universities, who no doubt recognized that they could continue to maintain their own position in the academic and indeed the social world without explicit participation in this agenda. But what Dearing (and the Jarrett Report) both did was to impose upon universities a quasi-democratic ethos of collusion with the values of a market economy. Under the umbrella of the principle that recipients of public money should be accountable to public scrutiny was included an explicit commitment to a particular form of public – a public which wholeheartedly endorsed the market.

In *Minima Moralia* the German social critic Theodor Adorno wrote of those whose lives are committed to the 'essential illusion of change' as a mask for the recognition of real social difference.[17] The expansion of recruitment to the universities is arguably an example of those changes which in effect bring about little or no real change, but nevertheless absorb and occupy huge amounts of individual and social energy. The creation of a significant sector of the labour market which can be described as 'graduate' does not in itself indicate any absolute increase in human skill, let alone human satisfaction. Moreover, the conditions under which that expansion has been achieved, the surveillance and standardization of the academy, have played their own part in the translation of universities from a degree of independence to a high degree of integration into the values of the market economy. To capture the shift in the quality of the experience of life in contemporary British universities we can return to Amis. Some twenty-four years after the publication of *Lucky Jim* Amis published a novel called

*Jake's Thing*, in which the subject is not the universities but the absence of middle-aged, male libido. But since the central character, Jake, is a university teacher we might read *Jake's Thing* as an allegory about the loss of vitality in universities themselves. Amis, by the time of the publication of *Jake's Thing*, was well established in his reactionary *persona*, and in his scepticism about the merits of the expansion of the numbers of students in higher education. Here the hero of Amis's novel, Jake Richardson, confronts one of his pupils:

> Now your spelling. I'm quite tolerant about that, [because a policy of being quite intolerant would multiply the failure rate by something like ten, which would never do] but the same thing applies. I know some of these names are difficult; even so, I think it might pay you for instance to remember that Mediterranean is spelt with one T an two R's and not the other way round. Especially [he went on, striving not to shake from head to foot with rage and contempt as he spoke and summoning to his aid the thought that in the Oxford of the 1970's plenty of his colleagues would share Miss Calvert's difficulty] since it appears in the actual title of the subject and is very likely to come in the wording of some of the questions – four times on this paper, in fact.[18]

The imagined student in Amis's fiction has moved from the hard-working Mr Michie of *Lucky Jim* to the less-than-enthusiastic Miss Calvert of *Jake's*

*Thing*. A generation of men – of whom Larkin and Amis are only a part – which attempted to claim the universities for their own find that these very institutions remain in the same (privileged) hand as ever but are now invaded by a popular culture that both preserves and disguises class. The attack on the traditional 'high' culture of universities has come, in Britain, from a complex coalition: left-wing modernizers, Tory pragmatists and all-party and all-class philistines. It is thus impossible to lay the responsibility for the transformation of the universities at any particular door: the wish to change and challenge the curriculum of universities is not an academic agenda with any clear parentage. During the years when Mrs Thatcher was Prime Minister it was clear that the Prime Minister had no interest at all in the idea of learning for its own sake; as the only Prime Minister in living memory to be refused an honorary degree by the University of Oxford there was clearly a recognition that Margaret Thatcher and the higher learning had little to say to each other. But at the time of writing there is little evidence that the British state under a Labour government is more enthusiastic about education for its own sake. That needy child of ill-matched parents, the contemporary British state, finds (in common with many unhappy children) that it is often difficult to concentrate on the difficult problems. The question of what education is, and exactly what it is for, has always been a difficult one to answer. Rather than try and think through a coherent answer, successive governments clearly prefer to accept the pressures and the interests of the market. Resisting those pressures would require the exercise of critical reason, precisely the faculty now being marginalized by the new order of higher education.

In 2003 Jack Rosenthal adapted Amis's *Lucky Jim* for British television. In that adaptation Dixon's drunken lecture is re-written for the twenty-first century, and concludes with the words, 'we should fight in the universities for proper teaching and make our lives merry'. This re-writing of Amis echoes a plea made by Bourdieu for the definition of scholarship to be 'to play seriously'. He writes – with an optimism that cannot but appear doomed to disappointment:

> *Homo scholasticus* or *homo academicus* is someone who can play seriously because his or her state (or State) assures her the means to do so, that is, free time, outside the urgency or a practical situation ...[19]

Perhaps, for some academics, a degree of 'free' time, in the formal sense of time which is not timetabled, still exists. But the 'practical situation', in the shape of the impositions, expectations and regulations of the state, increasingly assail this freedom. It is not, therefore, that academics are necessarily teaching more than twenty or thirty years ago (although many are) but that the 'free' space that surrounded teaching is no longer, in any sense, definable as 'free'. In offices and lecture theatres that are nowadays costed for the purposes of internal budgets, academics confront State-constructed agendas of performance. The needy unstable child that is the British state of the twenty-first century has never learnt trust, and almost never practised cooperation. For this creature, only battery farming for the mind promises that reason will never escape to serve anything except the most avaricious and limited keeper.

# The Heart of Darkness: Audit and Compliance

I am enthusiastically applying for the lecture-ship. My efficient, independent and collective teaching methods can greatly enhance the reputation of your department. I competently transform lecturing and research into significant learning environments. I prioritise, manage and co-ordinate inclusive action plans to meet coherent and comprehensive targets. Currently my tutoring evaluates complex representations and formations of sexism, heterosexism, racism and class oppression. I train teachers to raise academic achievements by implementing equal opportunities procedures. I am dedicated to promoting stimulating approaches that are relevant to students' aspirations. I optimistically aid multidisciplinary reforms to research and lecturing strategies. I am ethically and morally accountable to giving great educational quality. I offer regular advice, pastoral guidance and curriculum information that develop pragmatic initiatives. Integrating student participation I encourage their academic, personal and social progress.

(Letter of Application, UK, 2001)

The primary task of a useful teacher is to teach his students to recognize 'inconvenient' facts – I mean facts that are inconvenient for their party opinions. And for every party opinion there are facts that are extremely inconvenient, for my opinion no less than others.

('Science as a Vocation', in *From Max Weber: Essays in Sociology*, Routledge and Kegan Paul, 1967)

The first quotation above was not written for a university satirical revue, nor on April 1st. It is a real letter (in the sense that it is sent in absolute seriousness) written in support of a job application in an 'old' English University. It is an illiterate letter, in the sense of the use of the English language, but it also suggests, particularly dramatically, the conceptual illiteracy of the culture of audit and assessment which now dominates English universities. This culture was introduced with terrifying fervour, from the beginning of the 1980s: some landmarks in its dark progress across the landscapes of universities were the Teaching Quality Assessment (TQA) exercise and the Research Assessment Exercise (RAE). Other notable innovations have been the introduction of what is known as 'bench-marking' (in which academic subjects are expected to establish exactly what a graduate in that subject should know) and internal audit (a means by which colleagues can police colleagues in their own university, in addition to offering their services for external policing exercises). Marilyn Strathern, George Ritzer, Norman Fairclough and Frank

Furedi have been among those who have taken issue with this practise of audit and assessment. All these authors have, in different ways, challenged the assumptions that under-pin and inform these practices: the critiques have been fierce, passionate and informed by experience of life in universities in Britain and the United States. In addition to these voices, the pages of the *Times Higher Education Supplement* (*THES*) ring out every week with the protests of academics against surveillance and policing. Very few academics would be prepared to endorse the value and assumptions of the new audit culture and the following comment, made in 2003, is typical of the views of many:

> British academics are being crushed by assessments of their research and teaching ... There was no resistance to the introduction of these Stalinist measures, least of all from the Vice Chancellors, all eager for their CBE's and Knighthoods, their reward for presiding over the destruction of a once universally admired university system ... The teaching assessment is also ludicrous. I remember inviting a leading assessor to give a guest lecture to one of my classes on a subject on which he was an authority. Since he gave one of the most inept lectures I have heard in my life, it is probably best that he sticks to assessing how to assess other people.[1]

These remarks were made by Michael Burleigh, a distinguished historian and clearly someone for whom the British audit culture had come to replicate elements of that totalitarian culture which he described in his work on Hitler's Germany. In the same issue of the *THES* Alison Wolf, a Professor at the University of London's Institute of Education, voiced the opinion that 'We should, by now, understand that universities can't produce completely "work-ready" employees any more than workplaces can take over education.'[2] Thus in one issue of the *THES* (and by no means an exceptional one) current government policy about the universities is found wanting in two ways: the definition of the purpose of the university and the means through which that purpose is to be achieved.

It would be possible to replicate the quotations above a hundred-fold. Apart from those somewhat furtive zealots who must, at some level, actually endorse the values of the TQA/Quality Assurance Agency (QAA), the RAE and a university/workplace alliance, it is difficult to name (or indeed encounter) champions of these practices inside the universities. But the secret brotherhood, and sisterhood, of assessors clearly exists, since without it the exercises of assessment (and possible punishment) could not exist. The horrible psychic reality of a TQA/QAA assessor is almost too awful to contemplate, but contemplate it we must if we are to have any hope of identifying this beast, for whom extinction is the least that can be hoped. First, we have to recognize (unfortunate though it may be) that being educated involves assessment and involves being judged by others. From the very first moment when we are told at nursery school that our glueing leaves something to be desired, or that our colouring in is better described as colouring out, we are expected to conform to certain norms and expectations. From the age of five to eighteen we make our way through a school system which, in Britain at least, is now endlessly beset by tests and goals of attainment. Over-testing in British schools has now achieved its own critics (and its own political reaction, in the form of the resistance by many teachers to it) but the same widespread public sympathy has yet to emerge for the idea of over-testing in universities.[3] Precisely because university education has, until recently, been the preserve of the few, it is futile to suppose many people will extend much sympathy to those who have manifestly passed the tests. The cultural lag which can still identify being a student with being at the Oxford of *Brideshead Revisited* is not easily persuaded of the problems facing academics.

The generation of students which is now at university in Britain is the first generation which has been tested since the age of seven. Testing has become something of a national pastime (for those of course for whom it is not already a professional career) in that schools, universities and the culture itself participate in the support, creation and transmission of tests about all aspects of human life. We test and monitor our weight, our health, our ability to parent and to form lasting relationships. The connection between a culture of appraisal, beset with the neurotic anxieties which this articulates, and the social facts of growing levels of obesity and personal instability is seldom discussed. But in this context we have to examine the connection between this increasingly anxious culture and university practices.

It is thus that we need to try and enter the nightmare world of the university appraiser or quality assurance manager. (The situations vacant of all educational periodicals will demonstrate the widespread availability of these posts.) We have to assume (although it is sometimes difficult) that these women and men cannot be compared with the piano player in the brothel – these people do actually know that they are working in universities. But we have to ask exactly *how* it is that this fact will be known or discovered: given that through the manuals which assessors are taught to assess it is often difficult to identify the exact process which is being assessed. So we could perhaps assume that assessors choose their careers in order to make good the absence of God in a secular society. Judgement in the twenty-first century no longer lies in the hand of God: without this moral compass, however rigid it may have appeared, we enthusiastically create our own systems of judgement. The facile belief that a secular society is in some way free of the authority of judgement would be proved false by a day spent in a British university. Since God no longer exists, we have invented assessment. It is thus possible to imagine that the judging of others has become a new form of the democratization of God. Equally, the expression 'little Hitlers' might have a

resonance for many academics; despite its unfortunate anti-German connotations, most people
are familiar with the idea that there are some
people (be they in universities or any other
community) who simply cannot resist the opportunity to evaluate, judge and even reach the
paradise of the appraiser, the condemnation of the
appraised. Since contemporary academics are
now routinely assessed by their peers, their
students, their Head of Department and which-
ever external body happens to be visiting the
neighbourhood, the career opportunities for the
potential assessor are considerable. It is, in fact, a
growing sector of higher education and one which
offers a deeply rewarding career track for those
committed to judgement, and the assessment of
what is now known as 'performance'.

Western democracies have made much, particularly since the 'fall' of the Berlin Wall in 1989,
of the vices and cruelties of Stalin's Russia. These
same countries have also made much of that
reading of George Orwell's *1984* which sees the
novel as simply an attack on Soviet totalitarianism. 'Not like us' goes the refrain of these critics,
seeing in Orwell only a critique which endorses
the idea of the 'evil empire' of post-1917 Russia.
The 'People's Tragedy' – which Orlando Figes
has described as the history of post-revolution
Russia – was undoubtedly that; the second
tragedy of the descent of the country into greater
poverty after 1989 is also part of that history.[4] But
those interpretations of history, and literature,
which identify and associate totalitarianism and

authoritarianism *only* with state socialism, over-look and ignore the capacity of the democratic West for conformity and bureaucratic control. We might note that on 23 June 1931, Stalin decided that there should be an end to 'specialist-baiting':

> It would be stupid and unwise to regard practically every expert and engineer of the old school as an undetected criminal and wrecker ... Hence, the task is to change our attitude toward the engineers and technicians of the old school, to show them greater attention and solicitude, to display more boldness in enlisting their co-operation.[5]

On this, Joseph Stalin was some way ahead of contemporary British Prime Ministers and Secretaries of State for Education, for whom the idea of professional specialization, particularly in subjects which are not readily recognizable in terms of their part in the labour market, is a threat and a challenge. Most strikingly, academic subjects such as history seem to challenge the imagination of politicians. Although they are themselves products of a society which has been formed out of centuries of struggle for democracy and universal welfare it appears difficult for politicians to recognize that the world as lived in the late twentieth-, or early twenty-first-century Westminster is not the only possible form of social organization, nor that the problems which they face are not always unique in human history.

The greatest twentieth-century writer to have considered the question of the domination of the bureaucratic in Western societies is the German sociologist Max Weber. Weber recognized that 'modern' (that is twentieth-century) bureaucracy presented various kinds of problems, not the least of which is the 'dictatorship of the official'. The way out of this domination was, for Weber, politics – the attempt by individuals to communicate ideas of choice and difference to the population. Essentially, Weber hoped for a society in which informed debate – the practice of politics – could then be translated into social and political action by a bureaucratic machine. What he thought would actually happen – and for many people exactly what has happened – is that the bureaucratic would impose its construct of meaning and possibility on politics. In Weber's pessimistic prediction, bureaucratic discipline would become the dominant form of social organization:

> the consistently rationalised, methodically trained and exact execution of the received order, in which all personal criticism is suspended.[6]

Weber's account of the twentieth century has informed numerous studies of Western capitalism. Not least among these discussions has been the debate about the Holocaust. This discussion was generated by the argument of Zygmunt Bauman that modernity made the Holocaust possible: the ability (and impulse) to organize and control the social world, together with a sophisticated technology, provided the social means of genocide.[7]

The politics of fierce and obsessive anti-Semitism were imposed upon a social world which – as studies as diverse as *The Authoritarian Personality* and *The Third Reich* have suggested – accepted and endorsed a culture in which bureaucratic order was accepted.[8] The extreme example of the Holocaust is (very fortunately) an extraordinary case of the negative uses of bureaucracy but it should serve to remind us that the order produced by bureaucracy – and indeed its possibilities for fairness and social civility – is nothing without a politics to inform and motivate it. This can be achieved – although the achievement is always contested by those of the political Right who see only the democratic in a bureaucratic order – but Weber's own view, and that of others who observe the state of the twenty-first century, was that political goals would only be acceptable if translated into the bureaucratic norms of efficient, procedural rationality and technical skill. Weber was ultimately pessimistic about the part that politics could play in directing and defining bureaucratic order. His prediction was that bureaucracies would engulf the political, a prediction which invokes the prospect of spontaneous reaction. Those forms of reaction can take the forms of fascism or political ideologies which call for the end of 'state control' or 'nanny state'. All these apparently libertarian ideas are rooted in ideas about the rejection of 'control' and 'order', which might place them in a Romantic tradition were they not so often associated with extreme degrees of social conformity.

It is in this argument that it is possible to see an account of the modern world which precisely defines the current organization of British universities. The expansion of higher education is manifestly a political aim, and (at least in Britain) always a political aim of the Left. But that expansion has, in effect, been de-politicized by the way in which it has been carried out. The very bureaucratic structures which have been imposed upon universities have achieved both the devaluation of the eventual goal of a university education (the social and the intellectual value of a first degree) and the vision of democratic access and participation which informed the movement towards higher participation levels. There are more students in higher education (even if some of them are not in what is usually assumed to be a 'university') but public scepticism about what is achieved at the completion of that higher education has become considerable. At the same time, the world of the universities has become dominated by the achievement of bureaucratic standards and compliance with prescriptive standards. Whereas once all 'old' universities had considerable autonomy – and yet were remarkably similar in many of the standards of achievement – the new system of university policing has achieved further hierarchies within higher education. At one time there was little difference between universities outside Oxford and Cambridge, now Oxford and Cambridge remain one élite among other élite groups: the 'Russell' group, and the 'research-led universities' being just two examples.

Performance tables of all aspects of university life divide universities and, in addition to the usual fierce and vicious competition between individual academics, produce fierce and vicious competition between institutions.

Given that universities are supposed to contain the most astute and intelligent minds of their generation it is inevitable that questions should be asked about how this situation – of the double achievement of the devaluation and de-democratization of higher education – should have come about. One awful possibility is that academics, ourselves the products of doing-well-in-exams, could not resist the possibility of doing even more exams and tests and thus binding ourselves into an endless sado-masochistic tryst with the QAA, TQA and RAE assessors. This dark and hideous idea is not without a certain amount of supporting evidence. For over two hundred years various forms of comment have noted that the profession of scholarship can be accompanied by the most hideous pedantry and pointlessness. Comments about the final pointlessness of much of the activity of modernity accord easily with the fictional depiction of those characters such as George Eliot's impotent (in all senses) scholar Casaubon who devote themselves to a rigid version of scholarship. Eliot's portrayal of Casaubon in *Middlemarch* is tinged with sadness about the waste of human life and the loss of the capacity for human love.[9] E. P. Thompson, in describing twentieth-century scholars, was less charitable:

I have never ceased to be astounded when observing the preening and mating habits of fully grown specimens of the species *Academicus Superciliosus*. The behaviour patterns of one of the true members of the species are unmistakable. He is inflated with self-esteem and perpetually self-congratulatory as to the high vocation of the university teacher; but he knows almost nothing about any other vocation, and he will lie down and let himself be walked over if anyone enters from the outer world who has money or power or even a tough line in realist talk ... *Superciliosus* is the most divisible and reliable creature in this country, being so intent upon crafty calculations of short-term advantages – this favour for his department, that chance of promotion – or upon rolling the log of a colleague who, next week, at the next committee, has promised to run a log for him, that he has never even tried to imagine the wood out of which all this timber rolls. He can scurry furiously and self-importantly around in his committees, like a white mouse running in a wheel, while his master is carrying him, cage and all, to be sold at the local pet-shop.[10]

These comments, by a man who spent much of his life (although by no means all) as an academic, ring all too true. There is not, as yet, definitive ethnography about British universities in the twenty-first century, but the habits of *Superciliosus* are all too familiar to anyone who has worked in a university. That this is the case can be demonstrated by reference to the considerable fiction that presents universities, and the people who work in them, as often vicious, petty and self-seeking. Indeed, judging by the testament of fiction, universities are physically dangerous places; few other institutions inhabited by middle-class professionals have such a record for dead bodies. From the tales of Michael Innes and Dorothy Sayers about murderous goings-on at the Oxford of the 1930s to the equally lethal context of Carolyn Heilbrun's Harvard in the 1960s, universities are clearly not safe places.[11] Only a fool would walk to the photocopier without watching her or his back.

Thompson's image of the academic white mouse being taken to be sold at the pet shop has, sad to say, now an awful ring of truth to it since not only have universities committed themselves to the rule of the bureaucratic agenda, they have also allowed themselves to be bought by commerce, industry and the market. This purchase of the academic white mouse has taken two forms: the invasion of the culture of the university by ideas about 'enterprise' and 'the needs of industry'; and the literal purchase of university appointments or expertise by those individuals or institutions which wish to enhance their power and prestige. Of the two, it is arguably the first that is the more pernicious, since it is less explicit, more general and less easy to resist. Those appointments explicitly funded by wealthy individuals have been subject to considerable comment (and on occasions rejection by potential recipient institutions) but a culture of 'enterprise' is more difficult to contest.[12] Increasingly too, in the Britain of the twenty-first century, it becomes more and more difficult to challenge the very idea that universities should be engaged in 'enterprise' and 'links with industry'. The following comments by Charles Clarke demonstrate how the boundaries of debate have shifted:

> What I have said on a number of occasions, including at Worcester, is that the 'mediaeval concept' of the university as a community of scholars is only a very limited justification for the state to fund the apparatus of universities. It is the wider social and economic role of universities that justifies more significant state financial support. This is clearly a central issue for us to debate. It is why I invited Vice-Chancellors to a seminar with the confederation of British Industry and Patricia Hewitt, the Secretary of State for Trade and Industry. We started an excellent discussion about *how* universities can link in better with their local economies.[13]

The particularly chilling, and depressing, aspects of these remarks is that the word 'debate' has taken on a new, Orwellian, meaning to it: what Charles Clarke envisages as a 'debate' is of course a roomful of people with the same idea, working out how to put that idea into effect. Anyone who questions the view that universities *should* link in better with their local economy would not be enjoying the heady delights of a day out with the

Confederation of British Industry and Patricia Hewitt. But if academics want to resist the assumption that we should engage with the economy and the labour market, questions still remain about how we should make the argument. It is not enough, however much we regret it, to say that such an engagement is profoundly without intellectual interest.

We might, however, begin to make the case for the absolute distance of universities from the interests of the economy through asserting, far more loudly than has so far been the case, that the boundaries of the academic are very much worth defending, and worth defending because they constitute a set of standards and aspirations that are democratically available and can generally inform the social world about the possibilities of the intellect. Going to university to learn how to process received, bowdlerized knowledge (the hand-out culture of the QAA) is not about learning to think or consider. It is about learning how to organize pre-packaged information. A monkey could not do it, but then a monkey would not want to. This form of university education is 'democratically' available in the sense that considerable numbers of eighteen-year-olds (and others) can now enter university, but this is not about democracy any more than Charles Clarke's 'debate' is about disagreement and discussion. A democratic university education allows students to enter the system (and remain within it) with diverse aspirations and inclinations. Many may very well want to study mediaeval history, others may want to study how to be the best-informed graduate in social policy that New Labour could wish for. Democracy allows this, as it allows students to be taught in different ways and as it allows academics to pursue diverse, and even idiosyncratic, interests.

The 'ivory tower' of the academy was attacked in the past because it was perceived as irrelevant to the social world, and associated too closely with a caste of over-privileged white men. But that second association is important, because it should remind us that universities have in many ways remained servants of the same masters. Here then, the argument is not that universities should return to a golden, ivory built past, but that they should attempt to separate themselves more than has ever been the case, from the aspirations of the market economy. Until about 1970 (when entry to higher education in Britain did begin to become more extensive) British universities were partly about class assimilation: ensuring that generations (largely of young men) could continue to reproduce a particular culture. But in addition to this, British universities were about intellectual investigation, about daring to speculate and about affirming the possibility that critical inquiry had value. It is romantic to suppose that universities, and people in them, have dispassionately pursued truth. The history of intellectual life in the twentieth century demonstrates that many of the ideas that have had a transforming impact on our culture (for example feminism and psychoanalysis) have come not from the universities but from outside them. Nevertheless universities have allowed generations of students the space in which they can consider these ideas, not in terms of the difference which these ideas make to the world as a whole, but in terms of the difference these ideas make to other ideas. Ideally, what can be set in train by a university education is the ability to recognize the relationship between ideas, and how to evaluate them.

Learning in this way is light years away from the 'key skills' model of learning that is embodied in the expectations of the Quality Assurance Agency. This creature from the depths of hell is curriculum and discipline, blind: the content, the substance of a discipline is reduced to a resource through which students can acquire the means of demonstrating the 'key' or 'transferable' skills which will then be apparently 'useful' to the labour market. In reviewing the comments of an Associate Director of the QAA on the teaching of Social Anthropology Marilyn Strathern wrote:

> HEFCE's spokesman makes it explicit: skills must be disembedded ... However, by now the reader will not be surprised to learn that the skills have already been defined. The skills in question have to match up to certain expectations. Nor is it any surprise that – in certain respects – the expectations mimic the skills of audit presentation itself: clarity (rather than logic), itemization (rather than connection), bullet points (rather than paragraphs), and

simplified organisation (rather than involution or evolution in argument). Above all, not ambiguity, contradiction or hesitation.[14]

Strathern goes on to argue that where this model of 'learning' leads is towards the 'de-disciplining' of university subjects, and she cites the example of New Zealand's credit system of higher education which allows students to accumulate in a range of 'learning environments'. It is thus possible to emerge with a degree in that country without any substantive disciplinary training. As a choice about higher education, the New Zealand model could elicit comments about a little learning being a completely pointless thing. But for democracy to have any meaning we have to respect that choice about the means of higher education. Equally, we might want to preserve our rights as academics in a democracy and argue that 'key' and 'transferable' skills do not constitute a valuable form of education and that any model of education which is based on them should be furiously resisted.

# The Language of
Learning

In British universities all teaching is judged (by
a sort of spectral, invisible or scarcely visible
body of authorities) in terms of 'learning
outcomes'. As a teacher one is obliged to act
and feel like a sort of automaton, someone
concerned with 'deliver of unit' (rather than
'teaching of course') the outcome of which
should be specifiable in advance. Teaching is
becoming mechanized in a way that makes
caricature seem improbably realistic: Dickens's
Mr Gradgrind would have found it difficult to
believe. It is not only the teacher who becomes
an automaton, but also the student, for he or
she too is obliged to live up to the 'learning
outcomes' set down in advance, in other words
in a sense not to *live* at all, merely to 'receive
deliver'.

(Nicholas Royle, *The Uncanny*,
Manchester University Press, 2003)

Orwell was the greatest twentieth-century novelist
to make the case to a general audience: words
matter. Philosophers have long known this, and
long written about it, but George Orwell's *1984*

stands, for many people, as the definitive account of the way in which words and meanings can be abused and misused. The fictional world of Orwell's *1984* was hardly the first place in which words had been divorced from the original meaning: throughout the nineteenth and twentieth centuries, critics had noted the insecurity of meaning in concepts such as 'freedom', 'liberty' and 'progress'. These words, and others like them, had rhetorical possibilities which were not lost on those committed to social and political agendas. Orwell's attack in *1984* was on the annexation of the apparently secure meaning of words such as truth and freedom by those committed to dishonesty and enslavement. His agenda was political and his concern the removal of fixed meaning from language. Central to his case in *1984* was the argument that to lose the meaning of language we also lose our personal and social history; those living in a world without history have no mechanisms for the evaluation of truth and certainty.

It is tempting (and indeed irresistible) to move immediately from Orwell's *1984* to the publications of the Quality Assurance Agency and other agencies associated with learning and teaching in British Universities, since these publications illustrate particularly well all Orwell's fears about the misuse of language. The documents published by these bodies impose upon teaching in higher education (and the assessment of teaching) a set of ideas and assumptions which are (or were) foreign to many academics. What has been described as the 'technologization of discourse' in universities has established a set of principles about how to teach, the ordering of the curriculum and the presentation of knowledge.[1] It is the language, and the mind-set, of the late twentieth and early twenty-first centuries of the neo-capitalist ordering of the world. But two qualifications must be made: academics themselves have never been slow to use technical and/or obscure language and that 'technologization of discourse' described as a feature of the universities has, of course, occurred throughout the public sector of the contemporary British state. When rail passengers became customers and learning becomes 'knowledge transfer' there was a general sense that a certain erosion of meaning was taking place.

Orwell's attack on the misuse of language in *1984* is about the misuse of power, and the links between language, propaganda and totalitarianism. It is possible to write off the new 'language of learning' as an example of the misuse of power, and to assume that what has happened to language in contemporary universities is identical to the sad story of language in Orwell's Oceania. But to follow this argument would be to obscure some of the important differences between the worlds of Oceania and Universities UK, among which are different relationships to the market economy and different political aims. Universities UK are increasingly involved, and expected to be involved, in the profit-making activities of the market economy. Equally, power in Universities

UK is not about a 'boot stamping on a human face' which Orwell's character O'Brien describes as the dominant characteristic of the future, but a process no less about power, albeit power of a less brutal and more subtle kind. The corridors of academe do not echo with the sounds of torture; it is part of our own misuse of language that we talk about the 'torture' of committee meetings or the arrival of assessors, while forgetting the possible realities of the word. Universities have long been known as personally vicious and competitive places, but none of us in these Western institutions have been subjected to actual physical torture or deprivation.

Thus before slipping into an easy acceptance of Orwell's account of the future, we need to examine – the better to combat and question – the precise and detailed nature of the new world of learning. This world is not, like much else in the world, simply to be described as an 'Orwellian nightmare'. But it is, perhaps, a nightmare of a different kind, in which the horrors of force, violence, physical coercion and hardship, are replaced by the slow suffocation of the spirit, the intellect and the capacity to resist. We do not, as people who live and work in universities, have to confront daily expectations about making two and two into five, nor do we live in regimes of brutal physical force. But what we do live in has other resonances with Orwell's world, resonances which are often obscured by the more well-known brutalities of *1984*.

A major part of the thesis of Orwell's novel

concerns the extension of authoritarianism in the West. This is well known, as are the interpretations which suggest that Orwell's major target in *1984* is Stalin's Russia. From the days of his involvement in the Spanish Civil War, as part of the Republican Army, Orwell had maintained a deep suspicion and loathing of the politics of the Soviet Union.[2] While many of the British Left in the 1930s, and many in the population as a whole after the German invasion of the Soviet Union in 1941, they maintained sympathy for the USSR; Orwell was part of a small, complex and divided group which had, at best, deep scepticism about both the internal and the external policies of that country. That scepticism could align Orwell with libertarianism and the political credo of anarchism were it not for the argument in *1984* about the causes and the consequences of authoritarianism. What Orwell suggests in *1984* is an argument about the relationship of authoritarianism and equality, an argument which involves a discussion of authoritarianism but which is also related to the question of the complexities of establishing democracy without the eradication of difference and diversity. It is an argument which is at the core of *1984*, and indeed of *Animal Farm* and other writing by him. It is also an argument which is directly relevant to contemporary British universities.[3]

In Chapter Nine of *1984* Winston Smith comes across a book entitled *The Theory and Practice of Oligarchical Collectivism* by Emmanuel Goldstein. Winston reads this book in the exceptional circumstances – and for these reasons we, as readers, are allowed to participate in Orwell's reflections on the world of the future rather than being driven forward by narrative and events. In Goldstein's book an argument is suggested about the sources of late twentieth-century authoritarianism, a theory which proposes that authoritarian structures do not emerge out of nowhere, or indeed from conditions of material scarcity and poverty, but emerge in conditions of influence and the rich possibilities of technologically advanced society. Orwell/Goldstein writes:

> ... as early as the beginning of the twentieth century human equality had become possible. It was still true that men were not equal in their native talents ... but there was no longer any real need for class distinctions or for large differences of wealth. With the development of machine production, however, the case was altered. Even if it was still necessary for human beings to do different kinds of work, it was no longer necessary for them to live at different social or economic levels. Therefore, from the point of view of the new groups who were on the point of seizing power, human equality was no longer an ideal to be striven after, but a danger to be averted ... By the fourth decade of the twentieth century all the main currents of political thought were authoritarian.[4]

The passage hopefully gives some idea of the complexity of Orwell's argument in *1984*, an argument which is both more powerful, and more disturbing, than those assumptions which simply read *1984* as an anti-Soviet Russia diatribe. What Orwell is in fact suggesting is that all societies which become technologically sophisticated face very similar problems and questions about the organization and the distribution of social power. Readings of *1984* which locate the argument solely in terms of Soviet Russia are, of course, deeply comforting for the West, but they ignore the strength of the case that Orwell is making – that authoritarianism, defined in the most general and pervasive sense, is part of the experience of both East *and* West. The brutality of authoritarian regimes is clear in *1984*, but the brutality which Orwell asks us to consider is not only about the awful brutality of physical torture, it is also about the brutal attacks on the human spirit of regimes which order and control the lives of its citizens. Orwell, in his own life a devout non-participant in religious matters, cannot couch his argument in terms of the loss of spiritual resources –'the soul' – in the contemporary world but he does propose a secular version of the argument advanced by his contemporary Evelyn Waugh in *Brideshead Revisited*. The argument is posed in very different terms by writers with very different politics: that the material world, however rich and powerful, cannot offer all that is necessary for a meaningful human existence. Orwell is far too much of a materialist to advance ideas about the spiritual richness of poverty, but in all his writings, from the years of *The Road to Wigan Pier* to *1984*, there is a noticeable seam which recognizes and validates the importance of the non-material in human life.

In the years immediately prior to the publication of *1984*, British society had been, and was being, transformed by the establishment of the Welfare State. Central to the rhetoric of that political project were the ideas of equality and general access to significant social resources, most notably of health and security of income. Those ideas have now become part of what is loosely defined as European Social Democracy. But one aspect of British post-1945 social policy which was not part of the commitment to equal access, and equality in a more general sense, was education. British educational policy had been established, not at the end of the 1939–45 war and by a Labour government, but during the war, and through the energetic determination of a Conservative politician – R. A. Butler. Thus the educational policy which dominated Britain in the post-war world was not one which took equality as its organizing theme, but one which was founded on *difference*.[5] With hindsight, we may comment that Rab Butler, far from being a champion of democratic access to education, was inspired by a rigid version of social hierarchy: the Butler Education Act of 1944 has often been hailed as an innovative reform of English secondary education, but today we might be more inclined to stress the class distinctions of Butler's plans for schools, rather than those changes (such as the abolition of fees for grammar school places) which were, at the time, more arresting.

The assumption, in the 1940s and the 1950s, that Butler's Education Act was part of the New Jerusalem of post-Second World War Britain suggests that social, and academic, hierarchy was still an unchallenged part of the social order and the national culture. It was not until the 1960s that the movement for comprehensive schools began to be widely known (and supported) and through it a challenge to the idea that academic aptitude could, and should, be decided at age eleven. The 'eleven plus' became the symbol of a hierarchical educational system, one which was deeply ill-fitted to the emergence of a more culturally class-less society. The disappearance of deference, a youth culture and the material prosperity of the 1960s contributed to the definition of the eleven plus, and institutional divisions between children, as anachronistic, socially divisive and out of step with the culture of the times. Many arguments about comprehensive schools and the eleven plus emphasized the psychic damage done to children by testing (and labelling) at the age of eleven; rather fewer arguments noted the private schools and educational crammers which were, in part, the consequence of the eleven plus. Those middle-class parents whose children did not pass the eleven plus had, to avoid the horrors of downward social mobility, to resort to paying for education rather than risking their children's future at the local secondary modern.

By the end of the 1970s most parts of England (other than those profoundly conservative areas such as Kent) had abolished the eleven plus and created out of existing schools various kinds of comprehensive schools. A climate more sympathetic to the idea of social inclusiveness as well as antagonism to formal institutional divisions between children created an expectation of absolute equality in educational provision. Every child was to have the same kind of access to the same kind of education and no child should any longer be labelled a 'failure' at the age of eleven. The brutality of the eleven plus system – pass or fail and absolutely no middle way or equivocal or graded result – fuelled the expectation that the institutional playing field of secondary education should be as flat as possible and do as much as possible to correct the different degrees of privilege with which children arrived at school. But by the end of the twentieth century various writers (for example the journalist Melanie Phillips) had started to attack the very idea that underpinned the culture of educational equality – the idea that all children were, at least theoretically, capable of the same kind of academic achievement.[6]

The revival of what might be described as theories of *'natural'* ability in debates about educational achievement in school were fuelled in part by the concerns of parents (and others) that teaching in schools was increasingly being geared to the lowest common denominator. Media attacks on standards in examination performance became widespread and scepticism started to become part of the general culture about the value of educational achievements. In the same decade, the

1990s, a similar kind of debate began to emerge in the case of the universities – namely the suggestion that university degrees no longer had any 'real' value and that the degree courses followed by students were some way short of rigorous. The infamous 'gentleman's Third' once awarded to the idle sons of the rich at Oxford became replaced by the more plebeian, but equally academically irrelevant, degree from the University of Nowhere in Particular.

Between these two degrees there lies decades of social change and shifts in educational policy. Yet what unites the two degrees – otherwise radically socially separate – is that both are essentially attendance certificates. In one case a young person spends three years being in residence, in another case a young person spends three years collecting and regurgitating course material. The second young person may have amassed a great many hand-outs and logged onto a lot of web pages but an essential element of academic life is still missing – that of critical engagement with a subject matter and its related literature. Being at university has now acquired a new meaning for the majority of students – a meaning which involves constant surveillance and constant demonstration of participation. The surveillance between teachers and pupils is, of course, mutual. Teachers are expected to record the presence of their students, and increasingly their performance when present, while students are asked to record comments on their teachers. Teachers then survey and assess each other, while those assessments are themselves subject to a process of evaluation. Winston Smith was able, albeit rarely, to find a comfortable armchair in which to read. Many university staff would no doubt be grateful to find that twenty-first century equivalent of a comfortable armchair. The general experience of life in universities is far more evocative of other experiences in *1984*, not least the sense of being constantly and remorselessly surveyed. We do not yet have cameras in offices, but the call by the present British government for more 'e-tech' learning suggests that a day might come in which the general distribution of packaged information becomes equated with teaching.[7]

The present language of assessment and surveillance in universities suggests a conceptual world in which it is taken for granted that it is acceptable to survey, monitor and to judge the process of teaching. About this new rhetoric learning two points need to be emphasized: first, that the *right* to assess, monitor and above all *order* the work of academics by others who are not academics was never debated. The invasion of professional space by non-professional assessors has not, of course, been confined to universities: all public sector workers have found themselves subject to scrutiny, a scrutiny validated by 'public' rights to investigate and assess. How the 'public' is constructed should, however, be made apparent: the word implies a democratic and transparent attitude to public services and implies the involvement of a range of citizens. In practice, the 'public' is often dominated by those most committed to the values of the marketplace and entirely pedestrian ideas about the function of universities. (For example, in a Teaching Quality Assessment exercise at the university where I work the senior member of the team was a one-time Tax Inspector whose major concern – after his much re-iterated comment that he knew nothing about universities – was the relevance of the teaching of social theory to the 'job market'. The only honest response to his question was to say none, but so deep was the fear and dread of the exercise that individuals suggested that reading Max Weber took a central part in the training of Tax Inspectors.)

On that occasion, it was not conscience that made cowards of us all, but fear of doing badly in that loathsome and deplorable exercise. Across the country other academics, people who have spent years on specialist research and cared with some degree of passion about it, have also had to adopt what can only be described as the Winston Smith position: telling a bunch of lies because the alternative is a bad mark, and a bad mark means, if not physical torture, then public failure and even more assessment and even more regulation. Moreover, the very process of assessment is legitimated in terms of reference to 'open-ness' and 'accountability'. To challenge this orthodoxy immediately lays critics open to the charge that they are in favour of, not the sensible spending of public money, but practices of secrecy and exclusion. Academics are given no choice about participation or collusion with this assertion of legitimate investigation and policing: words which suggest democracy such as 'accountability' are used as part of a one-way process of coercion. What is most evocative of *1984* in the practices of the QAA is that there is *no argument*. The 'right' process is established, the rules of the game sct, and what is then required are cooperative and consenting players. (To further this end, most universities provide what is euphemistically known as 'staff development' for academic staff, which in the main consists of further familiarization, and implicit endorsement, of QAA procedures.)

So the 'right' to assess is set up as a process which cannot be challenged, and to which there is no apparent legitimate opposition. The second issue which arises out of the new rhetoric of learning is that assessment and regulation is driven by a discourse of equality and democracy. The thesis is that all universities, and the work of all universities, should be investigated in the same way by regulatory bodies, of which the Quality Assurance Agency is the most important. Hence, in theory, Oxbridge, London and every other university in England should be examined in the same way. Indeed, in practice, the majority of universities are examined in the same way, and the legions of ex-Tax Inspectors and professional pedants tramp through lecture theatres up and down the country. It is a pattern which vindicates all the possibilities envisaged by Orwell in *1984*: the ideas of democracy and equality used as vehicles of authoritarian control. For authoritarian control, and authoritarianism, is precisely what this pattern of regulation is; moreover, it is a pattern which produces no positive good and cannot be said to achieve any extension of either democracy or equality.

Regulation of the kind now practised in English universities produces fear, and little else. The various regulatory practices encourage mutual surveillance and informal discipline; what is never achieved through these practices is innovation, creativity or intellectual engagement. The documents that have to be produced for assessment and audit are absolutely and entirely *idea blind*; it simply doesn't matter if the subject is making sand castles or quantum physics, since the curriculum is marginalized by the process. For example, the documents that have to be produced for the process of modularization (the collection of documents about a particular 'module' – or what used to be called a 'course') ask teachers to spell out the 'aims and objectives' of the module, and the 'learning outcomes' to be achieved. The important part of the exercise is filling in the form: it does not matter that the aim of the module is to make a perfect sand castle, and the learning objective is not to do it when the tide is coming in. The computer, or the human equivalent, into which this nonsense is fed, will not reject it but probably thank you very kindly for completing the 'learning material'.

It is this context of learning that the present government hopes will create a knowledge rich society. If we substitute various other words for knowledge we can feel confident that the objective will be achieved: nonsense, yes, bullshit, yes, but knowledge is probably extending our understanding of the word past limits of the most optimistic and relaxed kind. The substitution of the emphasis in the curriculum to how we know something, rather than on why we know it, is authoritarian in itself, but even more sinister is the issue of how academics have allowed the process of regulation to go so far, since in the very nature of current regulatory practices there is a radical challenge to the very idea of critical inquiry. Admittedly, assuming that all academics are open-minded lateral thinkers with a firm commitment to free thinking is not entirely possible in the light of evidence about the exclusion of women and racial and ethnic minorities from both the subject matter and the practice of the academic curriculum. However, there have been enough academics who have pursued difficult or unorthodox questions for us to ask the question about the degree of voluntary collusion by academics with an assessment culture.

The relative ease with which regulatory practices have been imposed on English universities suggests a number of possibilities. First, the possibility that academics welcome regulation and endorse its driving principles. Second, that academics have had no option in the matter and third – and perhaps most damning if true – academics cannot resist taking tests, however absurd. On the first, it has to be said that there is little evidence that the majority of academics welcome regulation. On the contrary, the pages of the *Times Higher Education*

*Supplement* regularly contain complaints from academics about regulation, and any group or individual who questions it can be assured of sympathetic support. For example, when a group of Professors of Economics at the University of Warwick took to task the assumptions and working practices of the QAA they were hailed as heroes of critical opposition.[8] The second possibility – that academics had no option except to accept regulation – is more difficult to assess. Regulation in, and of, the universities began under the Conservative governments of Margaret Thatcher and John Major. These governments had no particular inclination to invest in higher education participation and no visible commitment to the idea of education. Thus a devil's pact of continuing investment in the universities coupled to a rhetoric about accountability and relevance emerged: universities would not actually be deprived of all funds, but they had to agree to become agents of the market economy. Subsequent governments have increased funding to universities but have made little impact on shifting the rhetorical space within which universities work. Thus it has become a matter of routine for university departments to be asked about their 'entrepreneurship' and the 2003 government document on 'The Future of Higher Education' was open about the need for higher education to harness 'knowledge to wealth creation'.[9] Harness is probably the right word here, given the regulatory strait-jacket imposed on British universities. But the understanding is deeply flawed: knowledge and wealth creation do not go hand in hand, and no perfect fit can be achieved without imposing limitations on knowledge.

Eroding the meaning and the use of language is, as every dictator knows, an important part of re-creating a social world. The invasion of the academy by 'transferable skills', 'relevance' and 'entrepreneurship' is part of the creation of a new academic world – an academic world which is assumed to be more 'modern' than the one it replaces. This rhetorical agenda about – and for – universities is all too welcome to some academics and academic administrators, since it suggests that universities could become an integrated part of the social world, a world of decision making, profit enhancing and energetic social intervention. Maintaining the boundary between the academic and the non-academic world is not easy, and the seduction of the new rhetoric of learning is that it apparently promises a part in the matters and events of the wider social world. Rather than being sidelined to some social and cultural dead-end the universities are promised a part in that 'project of modernity' which is dear to so many hearts.

So it would be wrong to assume that all academics have resisted testing and regulation in either the practical or the rhetorical sense, or questioned the problems and implications of the academic affinity with tests and competition. We become academics by doing well at tests (even if those tests are given more ponderous, and more pompous names of 'schools' or 'finals'). Academics are therefore deeply involved in a 'testing' culture, even though the extent of the testing has changed dramatically in the past twenty years. More undergraduates are required to produce more written coursework than was the case in the past, but more undergraduates are awarded degrees on the basis of coursework alone, although the 'old' universities are more likely to continue to use examinations than the 'new' universities. The usual pedagogic explanation is that coursework allows students to demonstrate a greater range of knowledge and different skills from those required to do well in examinations. The question of who does well in examinations is also relevant here: those concerned with the gender differences in the award of first class degrees at Oxford and Cambridge have concluded that the examination system awards aggression, singularity and the ability to maintain a coherent, if dogmatic, argument. Male undergraduates, it is noted, are more likely to do well in this system.[10]

So the arrival of coursework as a means of assessment in the universities could be interpreted as a part of the partial feminization of the universities. That is, women have been recruited in large numbers into universities: as undergraduates, temporary and part-time teachers, support staff of various kinds and, of course, the cleaners and cooks who make possible the huge ancillary conference business of the universities. But feminizing the universities has gone further than this: it has involved the socialization of undergraduates into those skills traditionally associated with women, and women employees.

Those skills are skills about being reliable, cooperative and able to recognize different points of view. These 'feminine' skills are not far away from the skills which students are now expected to acquire at the same time as a knowledge of a particular curriculum: skills of meeting deadlines, producing presentations with other students (the much validated 'group work' of many teaching manuals) and the accurate précis of hand-outs of distributed material. The ideal undergraduate is today the student who attends all required teaching and hands in essays on time, the person who behaves as the perfect functionary of a bureaucratic world. For women, the paradox of the twenty-first-century university is that it appears to offer entry into a space once reserved for men. Yet once women occupy that space, we are required to behave as the 'good girls' who obeyed every social rule and implicitly accepted the authority of a male order.

Given this present emphasis on tidiness and conformity in the process of teaching it is perhaps not surprising that academics should so easily accept the onslaught of a culture of surveillance and control. We might also note that – as suggested above – academics just cannot resist a test, however ridiculous. After all, a test always offers an opportunity to do better than someone else, and to those of us who have spent our lives competing against others at the eleven plus, in examinations at the ages of fifteen, eighteen and twenty-one another test is simply part of the agenda of our lives. Moreover, tests (as evaluation and assessment) always offer the opportunity for those running the tests to punish their foes, or work off old scores. Not for nothing was the Teaching Quality Assessment exercise described as the 'revenge of the polytechnics'. Living a less privileged life than the old universities, the new universities dreamed of a world in which they would expose the corruption and idleness of the world of the dreaming spires. A dream doomed to failure, since the new universities had failed to recognize the old feminist/socialist slogan, Nobody with Power Gives it up Easily. The 'good ole boys' in the old, and oldest, universities might have seemed to be comatose in dreams induced by long lunches and dinners, but they had no difficulty whatsoever in turning the new world of assessment and evaluation to their own advantage.

So the introduction of testing and evaluation as part of a project of the democratization of the universities demonstrated, yet again, that privilege is not easily given up. The meritocratic hopes invested in the TQA, QAA and RAE came to little when confronted by the institutional intelligence of the powerful − and, of course, the ludicrous nature, especially in terms of the language and concept, of the tests themselves. But one feature of the relationship of academics to tests has become clear in the past twenty years: as academics we cannot avoid assessment and testing, but we have to recognize some of the complexities of our relationship to this process, and the way in which the process can strangle creative and original work. Thus a further (chilling) explanation about the acceptance by academics of testing emerges, that academics actually enjoy the process of evaluation and assessment. In a profession largely divorced from day-to-day social power, 'testing' and examining is the point at which academics suddenly have a glimpse of power as impact-on-others. In the balmy days of May and June, British universities became the places in which fine distinctions are made between the work of different undergraduates: to the victor the spoils of the first class degree, to the vanquished the third class or pass degree.

This annual testing ritual/ritual of testing has, of course, now been replaced by a year-long cycle of testing. Tests, of one kind and another, dominate every week of the academic year, be they tests of the students or of the staff. In this way the academic world is transformed into a highly sophisticated testing machine: there are committees to monitor the testing (for example the 'Teaching and Learning Committee') and administrators whose jobs are devoted to the collection of material about testing – or, as it is more usually described, 'evaluation'. The academic machine has to be assessed on an almost daily basis, and there are very few aspects of the process of running a university which are now free from surveillance.

Except, of course, what could be described as the core function of universities – the passing on, from one generation to the next, of a particular set of ideas and the ability to understand them. This is not about 'learning about' or 'acquiring familiarity with' those 'key concepts' so beloved of the handbooks of the Teaching Quality Assessment, but it is about gaining the ability (patchy as it might be for all of us) to find our way through complex intellectual systems and make some sense of them. Learning in this way does not guarantee the same 'outcome' for every student; it is a far more anarchic process than the QAA's expectations about learning, in which 'key outcomes' are not only expected, but required, of teachers in the academy. Teachers, in this rigid pattern, are reduced to individuals who package, contain and make available ideas. Because we are required to state what students will learn – in the insane summaries of the curriculum demanded by 'modularization' – it is inevitable that teaching itself becomes ever more vigorously and narrowly defined. Academics always provided reading lists and summaries of particular courses, but the change in the past fifteen years is to outlines of those same courses which are entirely prescriptive in their outcomes.

We all hope, as people who fly in aeroplanes and become ill, that the people who fly those planes and administer the medicine have followed certain key courses and not been absent from the lecture theatre for basic aerodynamics or the germ theory of disease. But the skills necessary for technical competence are not the same as those necessary, indeed essential, for intellectual creativity or understanding. Moreover, it is a basic misunderstanding of science and technology to assume that learning in these subjects necessarily follows a mechanistic pattern. The sad truth is that the authors of assessment want the world, and indeed everything we might possibly know about it, to be organized into the bite size portions of mass catering. The standard potato chip becomes the standard idea, it has measurements and it has contours and nobody will be given one that is a peculiar shape or made of different materials. Given that mass catering also depends upon 'portion control' we can also expect that no one will receive more (or less) 'knowledge' than anyone else.

Diversity in chips (or fast food in general) has now attracted a considerable literature, from the attacks on McDonald's to the more general critiques of the relationship between fast foods and their demands for raw materials, and relationships between the First and the Third Worlds. But it is for good reason that George Ritzer, the high priest of the process he describes as 'McDonaldization', has also attached this label to the organization of contemporary universities, particularly in Britain and the United States.[11] The key elements of McDonaldization are, as far as Ritzer is concerned, efficiency, calculability, predictability and control; all ideas derived (not unproblematically) from Max Weber.

This account calls into question the claim of the universities to continue to be social sources of independent thought. It is not necessary to validate a rosy picture of the past of the universities to recognize that what is emerging is, in the main, a shift of the definition of function. This does not mean that all academics in all universities have abandoned or been forced to abandon the aspiration of critical thinking, but it does mean that the universities have had to come to various kinds of terms with an enforced marriage with the market economy, but perhaps as significantly, the monolithic values of a contemporary world. The Western world is today more liberal about certain kinds of personal behaviour than ever before in its history, but at the same time it is possible to detect greater social authoritarianism. The sociologist Mike Brake published a paper of which the title was 'I may be a Queer, but at least I am a Man'.[12] Today we might amend that title to say, 'I may be gay, but at least I'm an ideal functionary'. As the boundaries between the socially integrated and the socially excluded become more entrenched, and in some ways more difficult to cross (as evidence about social mobility in the West suggests), so it becomes increasingly important for those who are 'integ-rated' to conform exactly to certain kinds of expectations and standards.

The forces which have shifted universities towards authoritarianism in both practice and ideology have been many and complex, as have been the changes that have produced greater standardization in a world which has become in some ways more plural and more democratic. Academics cannot now, any more than in the past, take on the world, but we are still able to exercise some control over the world in which we work. An initial resistance, which might attract great popular support, and have important and beneficial consequences, could be a refusal of the language now inflicted upon university staff. Out would go consumers, mission statements, aims and objectives and all the widely loathed, and derided, vocabulary of the contemporary university. In could come students and reading lists. Hardly rocket science, but a demonstrable shift towards a clear definition of purpose, not just of universities themselves but of the idea that words matter.

# Gendered Spaces

In 1938 Virginia Woolf published her onslaught on male institutional power, *Three Guineas*.[1] The book is illustrated with photographs of the male great and good, dressed up as judges, generals, archbishops and members of universities. In 2003, lest we forget, no woman has ever dressed herself up as a general or an archbishop and very few as judges or heads of universities. Woolf's identification of power is with the summits of institutional power; not for her concern with the number of women who enter a profession, or occupy its middle ranks. Her interest is in occupants of the most senior positions within given hierarchies. But that interest is not formed simply in terms of the sex of the most powerful in the land; it is about the issue of war and peace, and who makes the decisions that lead to the former. Woolf argues that in both Oxford and Cambridge research and teaching are dominated by the values of competition, aggression and possession and it is through learning these values that the nature of the professions is formed.

In *Three Guineas* Woolf makes connections between gender, knowledge and politics that were forged out of her own experience of the rise of European fascism in the 1930s, the death of her nephew in the Spanish Civil War and the sense of the possibility of greater conflict in Europe. Connections between women and pacifism had existed long before Woolf wrote (for example in the work of Vera Brittain) but Woolf's agenda in *Three Guineas* was as much to identify the *genus* of war as to react against it. Finding the origins of war in the self-serving determination of the powerful to stay powerful Woolf then asks how women might best resist war, and prevent it taking place. Her answer is the outsiders' society – a group which will not collude in any way with war, and whose chief characteristic will be what Woolf describes as indifference. As Woolf writes:

> In the first place, this new society, you will be relieved to learn, would have no honorary treasurer, for it would need no funds. It would have no office, no committee, no secretary; it would call no meetings; it would hold no conferences ...
>
> On the other hand the next duty to which they would pledge themselves is ... To maintain *an attitude of complete indifference*.[2]

The italics above are mine, although the idea is central to Woolf's overall thesis of the importance of women refusing to encourage, support or in any way help to maintain men's wars. An 'attitude of complete indifference' is a form of resistance which undercuts the pompous and the self-important; if no one cares about your behaviour and your actions then both lose their social and rhetorical power. So it might be, Woolf suggests, in contexts other than those in which men lead other men to war, and expect women to grieve and tend the wounded. Those other contexts are those other institutions – the church, the universities, the judiciary – from which women have been excluded. Consider, Woolf says to women, exactly what you are doing when you ask to join them. She writes:

> Who can say whether, as time goes on, we may not dress in military uniform, with gold lace on our breasts, swords at our sides, and something like the old family coal-scuttle on our heads... On what terms shall we join that procession?[3]

By the beginning of the twenty-first century it is apparent that women in all Western, industrialized societies are eager to join those processions which lead to institutional power and reward. Indeed, the education of women, given the work of such luminaries as Amartya Sen, has become the *sine qua non* of a 'modern' society.[4] To educate women, at least to secondary school level, provides the most effective form of contraception that exists and allows women to escape from the most brutal forms of patriarchal control. To this recognition Woolf would offer only support; her argument is not with education *per se*, but with the assumption that certain kinds of knowledge are in themselves forms of power, and that those forms of power do little except support the powerful.

These arguments about gender and knowledge

(and the gender of knowledge as much as knowledge about gender) lead us to the issue of gender
in contemporary universities and the implications
– if indeed there are any – of the greater number
of women who now attend university. The fact
that the proportion of women undergraduates is
the same as that of men is consistent across the
West. What is equally consistent is the accom-
panying fact that men hold the majority of the
senior teaching and administrative posts in universities. Although men and women have been
attending universities in (almost) equal numbers
for almost two decades, this has made little impact
on the gender relations within universities: both
women and men are students, but the curriculum,
in terms of the subject matter and the people who
deliver it, is dominated by men. Women attend
university (as do men) because of the shift
throughout the West to a labour market in which
graduates are, in many cases, more welcome than
others, but aside from this instrumental reason,
questions remain about what is taught at university, and how this – to follow Woolf – produces
not *more* independent and critical thought on the
past of women, but less.

Anybody who works in a university is familiar
with the gender relations at work which have been
immortalized in the column which Laurie Taylor
writes in the *Times Higher Education Supplement*. In
that column, located at the not particularly
fictional university of Poppleton, much of the work
necessary to the continuation of the university, and
the academic department, is performed by the hard

working secretary Maureen. Indeed, in this case 'hard working' scarcely does justice to Maureen's contribution. Maureen is always at work, when at work she is always in her office, and when in her office she is always fully aware of what is going on. As the academics stagger through their days in a haze of confusion, either internal or external, Maureen is always on hand to deal with student questions, the intricacies of assessment documents and the running of the department. A few academics take the managerial shilling and become the authors of complex business plans but in the main it is Maureen, for a salary which is probably half that of most academics, who literally services the academic world.

Universities are not unique in their dependence on Maureen and her sisters and throughout the country, and indeed the world, there are armies of Maureens who scrub and clean, cook and type, care for children and nurse the infirm and generally allow the world of power to proceed on its way. Barbara Ehrenreich is among those writers who have pointed out the relationship between women created by the entry of women to the professions and other high paid forms of employment: to do this professional women need domestic support and it is from women that this support comes.[5] But that support, and the support which Maureen and others provide, is officially seen as 'women's work' and thus paid at rates that are below those offered for 'men's work'. Yet in going to university, and in acquiring the degree and the professional training, what women are taking on is a complex bundle in which they have been allowed into a man's world and yet will never be able to compete within it except through the greater social and ideological distance between themselves and the women who support them.

Moreover, while the above could be read to suggest that the professions now warmly welcome women it remains the case – some sixty years after the publication of the *Three Guineas* – that the Church of England still refuses to allow women to be bishops and women's position in the military is still only that of the non-combatant. We may not be in favour of the hierarchies in which bishops and generals appear but it is impossible not to observe the partiality of the permission given to women to enter the world of institutional power. Many people would no doubt rejoice at this refusal to allow women to fight, seeing in it determination to maintain femininity. But we might also see in this decision (and likewise the ruling of the Church of England against women bishops) precisely those ambiguities about women and power which concerned Woolf in *Three Guineas*. The Church of England, like the military, has no objection to women being employed in subordinate positions – how nice and convenient to have kind, gentle women variously looking after people – but what both institutions object to is the idea of women being in power. One conclusion – again as Woolf knew – is that women should fight against this exclusion and campaign for full access to institutional power. The other answer – and the answer which Woolf much preferred – was that women should refuse to participate in those institutions which refused women. Woolf's argument was that in seeking inclusion women validated the very structures which sought to maintain hierarchical power.

This argument – this advocacy of the refusal of collusion – is deeply attractive, if only because it introduces into a discussion of institutional life a recognition of the purposes of institutions themselves which is sometimes overlooked. Equally, it has to be said that the choice of the refusal to collude is more easily made by a world-famous and financially independent novelist than any of us more ordinary mortals, for whom institutional advancement offers, along with the cost of collusion, increased financial reward. Equally, for many years working in public institutions in Britain seemed to offer a form of public service: to teach, to work in medicine or the law offered work which contributed to the public good and was, for many people, attractive for precisely that reason. Thus both women and men might recognize Woolf's attack on the pomposity and self-serving nature of public institutions but there remained the consolation that the work being done within that context had some connection with values about a wish to heal or educate.

This concept of public service changed in Britain during the long night of Thatcherism. For various biographical reasons Mrs Thatcher manifestly loathed universities and indeed the very idea that work could in some way be engaged in without reference to the market economy and the profit motive. Whoever the Oxford don was who sneered at the youthful Margaret Roberts, and dismissed her as a dreary provincial drudge, has a great deal to answer for: Margaret Roberts, in her later incarnation as Mrs Thatcher, repaid that careless Oxford snobbery tenfold. Universities, schools, the judiciary and medicine, the very institutional framework of the liberal state, were to be brought into line with the private sector and expected to do their bit for the Gross National Product. Oxford University could, of course, fight back, and refuse Mrs Thatcher the traditional accolade of an honorary degree just as its very many other powerful graduates could undermine the Thatcherite enterprise. But other, less powerful, universities and institutions were less able to deliver either symbolic or real resistance: the loathing of universities created through the experience of social marginality was to wreak its revenge not on the powerful but on the less so. Thus other universities were brought into a framework epitomized by the Jarrett Report of 1985, a framework which specifically expected universities to contribute to the entrepreneurial skills of the nation.[6] From that day, every academic in the country was expected to be able to show 'enterprise' in the exercise of his or her profession, and once 'enterprise' had entered the university curriculum so could a whole new language of 'budget holders', 'business plans' and 'cost effectiveness'.

This language of private sector managerialism

has, as all academics know, been embraced with often idiot enthusiasm by the Vice Chancellors of English universities. This group of people, certainly of the same gender as those in the *Three Guineas*, embraced the corporate model in the 1980s in the hope – so they argued – that this would preserve some of the independence of the universities. (It is, of course, entirely conceivable that many Vice Chancellors actually approved of Mrs Thatcher's views about the world and the universities but in the main this hypothesis has been seldom explored.) Anxious to legitimize themselves in the face of Mrs Thatcher's determination to wipe anything approaching an independent (that is, not related to profit) thought off the map, universities signed up for an agenda of managerialism and 'modernization'. Linda Ray Pratt has pointed out that the new 'narrative' of education is a transatlantic phenomenon and one in which all universities are expected to endorse a profit and loss account-value to the economy and the ability to enhance world-wide competitiveness.[7] Various voices, Richard Johnson, Norman Fairclough and Earl Shorris, have attacked what Richard Johnson has described as the 'culture of the corporate boast' and no academic will have escaped the negative comments about this new culture which now fill university common rooms and the pages of academic journals.[8] Most tellingly, Norman Fairclough has used the phrase the 'technologization of discourse' to describe the process whereby what is done in universities is changed by the words used to describe it into another process and practice.[9] This transformation is so subtle that it is difficult to detect on a day-to-day basis (since students still go to classes and lecturers still teach them) but transformation it is.

The precise nature of this transformation of practice in universities is most clearly apparent in the social sciences and the humanities, where teaching methods have always been more discursive than in the natural sciences. The elements of transformation which can be identified are a gradual shift towards the 'packaged' lecture (that is a lecture reproduced on the Web or in a printed hand-out) and a set of learning 'aims and objectives' for every subject taken. The 'good' student can then match the aims and objectives to the material distributed and, as if by magic, a 'good' degree will result, which will demonstrate that the department concerned has 'added value' to the student it initially encountered. It is a model of learning which is as absurd as it is authoritarian, but its form (the mechanical distribution of information and its assessment) is essentially a game of match the numbers, albeit economical and ideal for the higher education of large numbers of undergraduates.

This new world of learning, a new world which it should be emphasized has been brought about by the collusion of Vice Chancellors throughout Britain, has initially apparently far more in common with George Orwell's *1984* than with *Three Guineas*. But this new world has characteristics which make *Three Guineas* still relevant – characteristics concerning the gender relations of universities, the use of women as evidence of modernization and the place in the social world which universities occupy. Woolf had identified the relative poverty of women's higher education in *A Room of One's Own*: the stewed prunes of the women's college which Woolf described have now disappeared at Oxbridge as the majority of colleges have become coeducational and women have access to the wealth of the men's colleges. But while these material circumstances have changed, Woolf, in both *A Room of One's Own* and *Three Guineas*, was arguing a case which was about more than the standards of institutional cookery: it was about gender and access to knowledge, and access to determining the authority of what is known.

The stewed prunes of *A Room of One's Own* are the most vivid example of the way in which the experiences of women and men undergraduates differed in the 1920s. Even so, Virginia Woolf was well aware that complaints about the quality of food derived from privilege:

> There was no reason to complain of human nature's daily food, seeing that the supply was sufficient and local-miners were doubtless sitting down to less.[10]

This kind of experience is unlikely to be replicated in the twenty-first century: women and men share the same food and there are few material differences in the situations of male and female students. But consider other kinds of occasions: the Freshers' Week or the Away Day or the Graduation

Ceremony. At all these occasions the general pattern of male/female academic relations will have changed little since Woolf's day: men will control the symbolic space, 'give' the degrees (and be awarded the honorary degrees) and represent the authority of the world which students are about to leave, or enter. Women may be scattered among the academics (and scattered and scarce we are) but our major function will be supportive. It will be women who pour the teas, collect the coats and organize the seating. The Maureens of the academic world will have sent out the invitations and dealt with the enquiries, but it will be Sir, the Chancellor, who will be thanked for the splendid occasion.

Anyone who has supposed that universities have now become open and inclusive institutions should attend a Graduation Ceremony or even a departmental Away Day. These latter occasions – much loved in the new corporate world as a way of passing on ideas about the institution's or the department's 'mission' – invariably provide that snapshot of the social world which visitors from Mars value so much. The occasion may well be held away from the institution so that staff, disorientated by unfamiliar locations for the lavatories and carparks, will be less ready to engage in critical discussion. The location is likely to be a chain hotel which makes much of its income from away days, and training days. Inevitably academics are welcomed by smartly dressed young women whose function remains that of the air hostess before she became a member of the cabin staff – to make men feel at home and to reassure them that all domestic services which they might require are fully available. The visitor from Mars will wonder why all these people have driven (or been driven) to a location at some distance from their workplace in order to be told things about that world, but the visitor's astonishment may only increase when the real business begins. That business will consist of the presentation of information on a screen, which the presenter will then *read*.

Our Martian will presumably be baffled by this process, since people whose business is reading and writing are now being treated as if they can do neither. When the presenter has finally finished reading the words on the screen (words which are often helpfully reproduced on a piece of paper as well) he or she will be thanked for the 'very useful presentation' and the group will be allowed food, drink or possibly a retreat to 'small groups'. At the end of the day all participants will be thanked for the 'very useful contribution' which they have made and they will depart little wiser and certainly baffled by the idea that they might have contributed to an agenda which had already been agreed. 'Old' coercion in the universities took the form of the more junior staff being told what to do by the more senior; the 'new' coercion takes the form of the imposition of a general assumptive world (and language) which it is impossible to challenge.

The new world of the universities is invariably presented, to students and the public, as a world

in which women participate equally. As undergraduates this is now the case, but in all other
ways universities remain the preserve of both men
in a literal sense and masculinity in the more
general sense. The majority of Vice Chancellors
are male, as are the majority of Professors and
senior administrators. This discrepancy is a matter
for equal opportunities committees and concern
about the issue rests upon the assumption that the
world of the universities would change if women
were to play a larger part in it. To date, the
evidence suggests that women who choose to
endorse the corporate structure of universities act
in ways which are entirely similar to those of men.
Indeed, even those groups which have some
interest in maintaining a sense of gender difference
are as demonstrably willing as others to collude
with the expectations of the audit culture of
learning. For example, the draft bench-marking
document of the Women's Studies Network talks
about a 'variety of forms of assessment in order to
encourage the acquisition of a range of subject
and transferable skills. Assessment strategies
should be explicitly related to learning outcomes. . .' The empty verbiage of bench-marking
is further reiterated to include the pious hope that
the student would be 'reliable, resourceful and
responsible in learning'.[11]

That sentence reads like a recipe for intellectual
conformity and good behaviour in a closed
institution. Clocking in on time, our ideal student
will read what is given and in all ways behave like
a model employee, a role which women are all too

willing to embrace. Thus the new higher education takes women into its vice-like grasp: women are used to show how inclusive higher education has become while at the same time the traditional expectations of femininity – precisely those passive Angel-in-the-House tendencies against which Woolf so passionately reacted – are endorsed by the general academic culture. Indeed, the ideal student in the literature of the audit culture university is essentially female: here is an example of femininity becoming the most positive virtue of the twenty-first century – with the proviso, as Linda McDowell has so tellingly pointed out, that femininity is most valued in men, while least valued in women.[12]

Once we begin to think about connections between the academy and gender in terms of qualities such as masculinity and femininity it is possible to enlarge the discussion of gender and knowledge and move it away from those depressing tables of how many women are Vice Chancellors and whether or not women in universities can break through the 'glass ceiling' of promotion. We can accept and endorse the idea that no one should be denied promotion in any hierarchy on the grounds of age, race or gender without becoming embroiled in concerns which refuse to acknowledge or consider the contexts within which promotion is sought. The discussion of masculinity and femininity allows us to speculate about how women and men learn, in universities, to articulate their gender and how the institution's ideas of 'success' are deeply related to ideas which are derived from assumptions about gender. Indeed, the whole critical apparatus of the humanities and the social sciences is infused with gendered judgements: 'terse' prose is, of course, masculine prose, while 'flowery' was for some time an adjective used to suggest a confused femininity. New spaces within literature, the arts and the social sciences (the impact on Western culture of second wave feminism from the late 1960s onwards) has established new possibilities and new horizons for women writers and academics but within this increasingly plural and diverse culture there nevertheless remains institutional power, and institutional power which is as implacably masculine, in its direction and its assumptions, as it was in 1938.

To illustrate how little has changed in the way our public life and our knowledge about the world is constructed it is only necessary to study the dynamic and the rhetoric which surrounded the invasion of Iraq in 2003 by Britain and the United States. On both sides of the Atlantic political leaders, George Bush and Tony Blair, adopted the self-consciously determined stance of men divorced from ordinary, civilian ambiguity. Tony Blair had won two elections because he managed to convince a public (and particularly women) that he was a man open to the possibilities of the feminine: male power was disguised in the new cloak of feminized masculinity. But that role became unsuitable once war became possible; now the public world demanded an absence of ambiguity and a view of politics which divided, as Blair said, the world into camps of those who are for us and those who are against us. In the United States George Bush had less subtle games to play; the ever ready war culture of the United States was all too willing to take up those neat, and profoundly stupid, distinctions between right and wrong.

The war against Iraq in 2003 was, it is important to stress here, about many factors as much as sexual politics in Britain and the United States. The attack on the World Trade Center, the commercial rewards made possible through access to new oil fields, new consumer markets and political ambitions for Western control of the Middle East all contributed to the enthusiasm of the Bush government for war. But what was remarkable about the war – deeply unpopular as it was in Britain and Europe – was the re-emergence of public, masculine certainty in the person of Tony Blair. It is this sense of certainty, and of right to certainty, that was so much a part of Woolf's argument in *Three Guineas*. When Woolf parodies the attempts by men to demonstrate first the intellectual and then the physical weakness of women she notes sarcastically the account given by men of women's brains:

> It was a practical brain, a pettifogging brain, a brain fitted for routine work under the command of a superior. And since the professions were shut, it was undeniable – the daughters had not ruled Empires, commanded fleets, or

led armies to victory; only a few trivial books testified to their professional ability ...[13]

Woolf makes clear that she is well aware that as she writes many obstacles to the education of women have disappeared. What she describes as the 'long and dreary list of those barren if necessary triumphs' enabled women to pass examinations, enter professions and occupy some of the public space once only the preserve of men. But the cost of this is, as she sees it, considerable. It is that argument, or a version of that argument, which we could now use to explore the links between Tony Blair, masculine certainty and the universities.

The universities – a far larger and more heterogeneous collection than they were at the time of *Three Guineas* – have now (as suggested above) been brought *explicitly* into the service of the state. The idea of the universities as 'ivory towers' is no longer, if it ever was, an acceptable or accurate account of higher education; the philistinism of the Thatcher years was part of the reason that universities were driven into a closer embrace with central government, but it was not the only one. Other explanations include the agendas of new universities, social engineers and longstanding antagonisms between the privileged and the less privileged within universities. Academics in new universities spoke with glee of submitting Oxbridge to the QAA regime; women enthusiastically endorsed processes which appeared to decrease the strength and the power of the old boy network. In the early 1990s it was sincerely believed that more 'accountable' processes of audit in the universities could reduce what was seen, by some, as unacceptable patronage and self-seeking. No one, at that point, had envisaged a House of Commons with more women in it then ever before endorsing an unpopular war against Iraq.

If we take the House of Commons as an example of the way in which institutions (and in this case a party political machine) can eliminate differences which appear significant outside those institutions, we can see how readily universities have been able to absorb women as students without making any significant concessions to the structure of power within them. But this integration of women has only been one aspect of changes that have been occurring in universities; hence women have become part of institutions which have themselves been changing in both structural and rhetorical ways. In structural terms, universities have been increasingly organized in terms of competition both external and internal. Universities compete ferociously against one another for funding; departments compete for funding within institutions because of new regimes of 'internal budgeting'. Hence an institution which might once have assumed that its physical space (lecture theatres, seminar rooms and so on) belonged to all its members, now charges individual groups or individuals for the use of those facilities. 'Successful' departments obtain, in effect, the gold paper clips, others make do with whatever they can find.

This world of endless financial calculation is not confined to universities; indeed it is a regime which has been enforced throughout the public sector. But perhaps more destructive of the academic world has been the new rhetoric of universities, in which, as Richard Hoggart has argued, there is increasingly little space for truly independent academic inquiry. Writing about the use of the word 'professional' Hoggart remarks:

> Most of these new styles of operators ... are not professionals, since they manipulate ... language for profits or other ulterior ends. It is a sad sign of their insecurity or just plain cheek that they cling to the word 'professional' to describe themselves. Since their ethics are never pure, always contingent on the need to deliver what those who pay them want (which is itself always and entirely contingent), their self-designed tickets of entry to the professions can never be honoured at the entrance gates. They are parasitic on and compliant to activities which are always disinterested, never interested.[14]

These 'new operators' within the university can, of course, be either male or female. Such is the beauty of the new managerialism that gender becomes irrelevant – all that the new managers have to demonstrate is that they endorse the ethics, the interests and the purposes of the new academic regime. Here is that aspect of *1984* which has often been obscured in readings of the novel: the recognition by Orwell that the creation of an all-powerful regime, with a non-existent civil culture, can minimize or reduce gender differences. Indeed, the actual experience of regimes such as Communist China and the old Soviet Union is that is exactly what happened: women and men became 'equal' citizens (and arrangements were put in place to provide child care) but men remained all-powerful. At the same time, although gender differences are not eliminated in the same way in Western capitalism, the demands of the capitalist workplace are such that gender differences no longer determine participation in that marketplace, even though they radically determine success within it.

Sociologists of work have long commented that both the private and the public sectors are increasingly anxious to demonstrate their ability to 'modernize' by employing women. Laura Flanders, in *Bushwomen: Tales of a Cynical Species*, has argued that in the United States, the administration of George Bush junior has used women, and female-friendly rhetoric, to secure the policies of the political Right.[15] Thus in the United States – and equally in Great Britain – bombing campaigns against the Taliban in Afghanistan were legitimated in terms of the 'emancipation' of women and the 'fight' for their freedom. Material about the rape and torture of women by Saddam Hussein's regime was used in a similar way: while no one would wish to deny the veracity of much of this material, what is questionable is the selective use of 'pro-women' arguments and the ongoing absence of any public, and governmental, argument which states the other case about the position of women through-out the world – that of under-paid and exploited workers. That case, made by feminist anthropo-logists, development workers and others, does not constitute part of a Western agenda for political and social change. Barbara Ehrenreich and Jan Jindy Pettman are among those who have pointed out the rigid, global, relationship between women and poverty.[16] Others, for example Mike Savage and Anne Witz, have argued that one of the iron rules of bureaucracies is that they are quite willing to use the skills of women, and demonstrate an enthusiasm for the competencies of women for cooperative working and what are often dubbed 'people' skills, but they are never prepared to offer women power.[17]

So women have been brought into higher education as what are now described as 'con-sumers' and allowed to take part in the bureau-cratic structures that have been created through the audit culture. In universities, middle and junior management is well served and populated by women, whose job is to check, to monitor, to report, to audit, to note and to process the monstrous mechanisms of the paper trails of higher education. The local and national bureau-cracies of higher education are staffed by women who provide the day-to-day organization of universities, in which, as M. L. Davies has suggested:

> ... current higher education culture ... is to

make balance-sheets sound like Homer and
Homer sound like balance-sheets ... British
higher education policy now turns solely on the
enforced internalisation of managerial control
mechanisms. Their intention is to displace
universalising intellectual comportment by
task-orientated technocratic procedures
through behavioural conditioning; to make
the experience of thinking and learning the
sterilised aggregate of specified technical
norms.[18]

'Behavioural conditioning' includes, of course,
learning how to act as a gender-neutral person
in a culture in which men remain powerful.

The new model of femininity of the twenty-first
century does not, at least in the West, refuse the
higher education of women or assume that women
will be taught in less privileged institutions. Yet
while women now have *access* to higher education,
what shows little sign of changing is the domination of the universities by the interests of the male,
public world. That world has changed in that it is
now formally expected that universities are
primarily about a contribution to the national
(mixed) economy. Thus while women once had to
seek access to universities, that barrier no longer
remains; in its place is participation in a world
which is expected to contribute actively to a
global capitalist agenda. The 'sign' of femininity is
now one which is used to suggest radical, 'people
friendly' change: an institution which accepts
women cannot, it is assumed, be all bad because

women still maintain that association with caring and altruism which has existed for centuries. Virginia Woolf's 'angel in the house' (a twentieth-century use of a term originally coined in the nineteenth) is no longer in the private house, but she is in every institution in the West, cleaning, processing, feeding and generally serving the interests of those institutions whose values and purposes she has played no part in shaping.

There is no reason to suppose that should the angels in universities be given a real role in determining their policies that those policies would be any different from those which now dominate. To think that this might be the case would demand the acceptance of essentialist ideas and endorse the expectations of those who value women as a 'sign' of modernization, but refuse to allow any real changes in the relative power, either social or intellectual, of women and men. 'Allowing' women into universities – for the same old paternalism which once grudgingly admitted women to degrees still persists in much of the sector – has a twofold impact: it allows universities to appear 'modern' and yet at the same time it maintains the *status quo*, and to a large extent arguably denies any awareness of gender difference.

Thus the argument here is that women, as students and staff (in all categories) of universities, have been integrated and absorbed into universities in ways which allow formal, institutional, knowl-edge (and its structure) to continue to disallow and ignore gender difference. Acknowledging gender difference is, on one level, about recognizing the

different priorities and responsib-ilities which
women have (and wish to have) outside the
university. These responsibilities – particularly in
relation to child care – are part of the lives of
everyone in any community but continue to impact
upon women's day-to-day lives in ways which are
well documented (indeed in the last twenty years
these responsibilities have been documented not
just well but exhaustively). In many accounts by
women academics of working in universities the
question of having (or not having) children recurs
frequently; one particularly poignant comment
from one of these accounts came from a woman
who said she was far 'too busy' to look after a
goldfish, let alone a child.[19] Contemporary institutions – as studies again show time after time – eat
people alive, and in particular demand of us an
absolute dedication to the workplace. Academic
work is by its nature endless; the perfect study, the
perfect explanation, the perfect book is always
waiting to be written. Place this specific imperative
alongside Protestant expectations about work as
the route to heaven and a noxious cocktail of
obsessive, workaholic values is created.

The new academy demands, however, not just
the dedication to the pursuit of knowledge of
previous epochs, it now demands the completion
of those new forms of regulation which have
recently emerged. Everyone has to comply with
these new regulatory devices; thus for anyone
whose time (and energy) is limited by concerns
outside work, the first priority has to be
compliance with regulation. Unless we comply

with the various forms of assessment (of ourselves, our colleagues and our students) we make ourselves invisible, yet at the same time vulnerable to complaints of non-participation. For reasons of social reality let us assume that the majority of people dealing with the coal face of the two lives of home and work are women and it becomes immediately apparent why women are not just *as* disadvantaged in contemporary universities as those of the past but arguably *more* so. As women we have been given access to universities, and in those universities success still remains, for academics, a matter of publication. The goal posts have not, therefore, changed, but the pitch is now so full of rubbish and junk that it demands enormous energy and skill to avoid it. To use another metaphor about games: the old game of snakes and ladders which was university life has now some new and far more deadly snakes. Instead of being called 'Sexism' the snakes – now more apt to swallow their prey whole rather than just sting them – are called 'Monitoring' or 'Objectives'. Old fashioned sexism never attempted disguise; the new managerialism is all about the subversion of language and purpose.

Day-to-day existence in contemporary universities can, therefore, fill the time of academics with purposeless activity, and activity which is unrelated to the promotion ladder. (At present no one has actually been promoted in a British University for the beauty of the prose of their module assessment, but that day may well come.) The

compulsion to take part in this meaningless circus
is general (the democracy of misery here is total)
but the compulsion impacts differentially, in that
those with more time have still time to do other –
more interesting, more valuable and more promo-
tion-related – things. This is level number one of
the new sexism in the contemporary university –
universal constraint, different impact. Level number
two is the complex level of the relationship
between gender and knowledge. If the 'mind has
no sex' it is nevertheless the case that some minds,
most of them in male bodies, seem to fare
considerably better than others. The reasons for
this – other than those of time and energy which
were raised above – concern those issues of the
centrality of some ideas rather than others, critical
opinions and gender, networks and gender and
other myriad issues of judgement, assessment,
evaluation and prejudice which constitute academic opinion. Some of these aspects of the
academy are clearly structural – the networks,
for example – and are relatively easily shifted,
replicated or challenged. Yet at the very core of
these issues is one raised by Woolf in *Three Guineas*:

> Do not merely sign this manifesto in favour of
> culture and intellectual liberty; attempt at least
> to put your promise into practice.[20]

Woolf had every confidence in, and was passionately committed to, the belief that women were
as capable of creativity (in whatever sphere) as
men. But she recognized the dangers and the
pitfalls of that fight for inclusion which has been so

much a part of the feminist agenda. In the case of universities women are now welcomed, even sought. Yet the world that welcomes us welcomes women as a sign, a sign that can be used to obscure the real prejudices and disadvantages that women still face. These prejudices and disadvantages are both structural and symbolic – structural in the sense that women are now included in a debased, but more demanding, form of academic life without any of the traditional support systems of men; symbolic in the sense that the apparent erosion of gender difference disallows the investigation of that difference and the radical discussion of the implications of gender difference which might result. Feminism (in common with socialism and psychoanalysis) is one of those great narratives of the twentieth century which originated outside the universities. Its involvement in the academy has opened up spaces for some women and some ideas, but at the same time that very academic space has increasingly taken a stranglehold on the imagination of its participants. To regain the imaginative possibilities of gender difference would now demand a new politics within the academy, a politics not about inclusion, but about, and in favour of, exclusion from those practices and processes which increasingly deform much of academic life.

# Iron Cages

The present government of Great Britain is committed to policies which would ensure that fifty per cent of every generation of school leavers enters higher education. Allowing for the possible slippage of the term 'higher education', which could, and does, cover a multitude of institutions and courses, this remains a considerable ambition without universal enthusiasm. But if something like that target is achieved it is worth considering the possible consequences of such a significant shift in the pattern of British post-compulsory education. Arguments have already been made about the decline in value of degrees and an increasing polarization in the labour market between those with, and those without, degrees.[1]

The range of degree courses now on offer in British universities becomes most publicly and comprehensively available in the middle of every August when universities advertise in the national press the vacancies which they have on offer. The traditional university subjects are represented, but so too are 'entrepreneurial skills' and a range of vocational degrees. What is most striking about this list of vacancies is twofold: first, that many of the most prestigious universities (for example Oxford, Cambridge, London School of Economics) are not even involved in this process of clearing and, second, the preponderance of vacancies at the post-1992 universities. There are no places at medical school (except at the University of Prague) and the more well known the university the less likely it is to appear in these pages. London and Oxbridge were always the first choice for many students, but what now appears to be emerging is a pattern in which universities have acquired a status not unlike that of designer clothes: no one wants the trainers without the right label, and no one at the beginning of the twenty-first century wants the degree without the correct designer paternity. George Ritzer and others have argued that the process of 'McDonaldization' is producing a situation in which all higher education becomes standardized (and standardized towards the lowest common denominator possible).[2]

But while this *might* be true of the curriculum – and is certainly true of the view of the curriculum dear to the understanding of the QAA – it is clearly not true about the universities themselves. Some universities – a relatively small group – are quite clearly more desirable in themselves, regardless of the subjects which students are reading. These 'designer label' universities were always attractive, but now they have an added quality of being not like, and indeed distinct from, other universities. The word 'university', which at the time of the Robbins Report had a considerable degree of descriptive homogeneity to it, has now been stretched beyond breaking point. No one simply goes to university any longer; students go to particular universities, among which some are manifestly more equal than others. It is apparent that the word 'university' is, in contemporary Britain, a vague and unreliable term. The loss of reliable meaning to the term is part of that cultural shift of the late twentieth century which saw the re-working of certain key words, so that they acquired a more socially acceptable meaning. Thus the 'market' (in the sense of an economic marketplace) became, during the 1980s, equated with the state of civic freedom; the fall of the Berlin Wall in 1989 and the demise of state socialism heralded an area of one tune politics for the West, that tune being the 'free' capitalist market as the only possible location for individual freedom.

This new politics of modernity came at that point when Western culture was commonly described as 'post-modern'. The central characteristic of this 'condition', as it is often named, was 'the decline of grand narratives'. The thesis, following David Harvey, John Jervis, Lyotard, Marshall Berman and others, emphasizes the diversity and the difference in human existence.[3] John Jervis has put the issue particularly (and typically) precisely and clearly:

> In effect, postmodernism is necessarily *not* restricted to the arts; it must necessarily both entail, and grow out of, 'post-modern culture'

more generally. In this context, it functions as an ideology of popular culture, culture in the age of mass consumerism; it proclaims the revenge of popular culture on the élitism of modernism, but it is a revenge that, ironically, generalises the insights and implications of the latter, the questioning of established forms and canons of representation ... One might say that if the modern way is to have relatively stable notions of group and personal identity, then the post-modern way is to multiply the margins and transitions: we all become betwixt and between, flows and circuits rather than fixed points in a moving world.[4]

Cultural pluralism is not just the new order – because unless we adopt an absurdly rigid and exclusive account of the past that was always there – it is an order without the authority structure of the past.

In education (and higher education is very much part of this theme) cultural pluralism has posed both, in Britain and elsewhere, considerable difficulties, not least because the understanding of the cultural transformations of the second half of the twentieth century has been, to say the least, limited. When Bill Clinton said of politics in the United States that the most important issue was 'the economy, stupid' he might have added that second most important was culture, and cultural transformation. Western society has been transformed by the cultural shifts of the past forty years (sexual permissiveness, multi-culturalism, the erosion of secure élitist judgements and so on) but politicians, and policy-makers, have been slow to grasp the implications of these changes. In the case of Britain the social triumph of popular culture has diminished some aspects of the cultural distinctions between social classes, at least among the young. But, and it is a but of enormous and important emphasis, access to, and understanding of, élite culture still carries with it considerable ease of access to élite institutions. It may very well be the case that sociologists of mass culture and gurus of media studies present detailed studies of David Beckham and the equal significance of *Eastenders* and *Middlemarch* but those cases and arguments are still made, and judged, within a set of expectations about literacy and a range of cultural reference. It is not therefore just that Beckham or *Eastenders* become subjects, they become subjects within, as John Jervis put it, 'the élitism of modernism'. Hence what appears to be a more inclusive academic subject matter is only that in the most trivial way; the actual framework of analysis, appreciation and the authority of argument remains embedded firmly within the complexity, the ambiguity and the often inaccessible world of élite culture. Above all else, this world depends upon literacy and an ability to use and understand language. It has long been noted that the natural sciences offer greater opportunities of social mobility for what used to be described as the working class. The reason was not hard to find – those subjects did not demand the command of English that the humanities and, to a lesser extent, the social sciences did.

In any culture words matter, as does what is done with words. The relationship between words, post-modernity and higher education is complex in that while the cultural pluralism of post-modernity has apparently opened up 'ownership' of the curriculum to previously excluded majorities (women and non-white people) it has maintained the evaluation and the determination of access to authority in that curriculum through traditional ways. Élite universities might allow the study of popular culture (although they generally allow not nearly as much of it as less élitist universities and hell will probably freeze over before Oxbridge allows a degree in media studies) but they do so while maintaining expectations about familiarity with a range of cultures and the standards and expectations of the modern quite as much as the post-modern. For these institutions, popular culture is not *the* culture, it is an aspect of the culture. For the majority of the population who live within popular culture, it *is* the culture.

For schools and universities, the emergence of explicit cultural pluralism is the great stumbling block of the twenty-first century. For the first sixty years of the twentieth century schools and universities could educate young people in a 'great' tradition which, if not as restricted as that of F. R. Leavis, was generally agreed. Children at those secure bastions of the middle-class world –

the grammar schools – were expected to accept
without a murmur the idea that the national
written and spoken culture was recognizable and
stable. Then a variety of impulses and values
began to question that idea from within: left-wing
writers such as Raymond Williams, Richard
Hoggart and E. P. Thompson questioned the
view that the goal of all great writers and thinkers
was incorporation into the British state.[5] Instead,
they suggested that many great English writers,
and many great English people, were actually
inspired by subversive ideas which emphatically
did not include the reproduction of the existing
social hierarchy. Put like that, a number of key
figures, and key literary moments, became part of
the history of social radicalism as much as the
history of English literature; the writers were
inspired as much by liberty, equality and frater-
nity as by the beauty of the English language.
Once this *genie* was out of the bottle there was no
stopping the re-writing of English cultural history.
The re-writing of the history of the English
working class was followed rapidly by the writing
of the history of women, of sexual 'minorities' and
colonial subjects.[6] Within the space of about thirty
years, a whole new social world appeared on the
curriculum and on the library shelves. As the
sexual revolution made possible new public
discussions of sexuality, so the rules surrounding
sexuality changed. For example, Stan Barstow's
novel *A Kind of Loving* was hailed on its publication in 1960 as an exciting departure in sexually
explicit literature. Forty years later few adoles-

cents would understand the meaning of the term 'shot-gun wedding' – the event which provided the book's conclusion.

So new explorations within culture gave birth to new rules and new forms of behaviour within that culture. The new British universities of the 1960s were part of this cultural transformation, even though some of them, with their organization into colleges and the adoption of arcane eating rituals, looked backwards rather than forwards. Most of this nostalgic educational organization was swept away in the cost cutting exercise of the 1980s but what has remained has been the uneasy relationship between universities and the culture of the twenty-first century. The rise of the entrepreneurial university in the United States has been condemned by its critics; in Britain attacks have been less on the entrepreneurial inclinations of universities than on their general 'dumbing down'. On recent trends in the United States one critic has written:

> ... to establish commercialisation as a 'key mission' of the university, on an exact part with its commitment to teaching and open inquiry, is crucially to confuse centre with periphery and to misunderstand what it is that universities can do which no other institutions in our society are able to do, or to do nearly as well. Basic research and well-educated (not just well-trained) students are public goods: goods which, unlike a seat at an Arsenal home game and like the beam from a lighthouse, are not

made scarce to me because you have access to them, and out of which it is, therefore, difficult to make a profit. And, as the Federal Reserve economists pointed out: 'Because these products are types of public goods, unfettered markets will fail to produce enough of them. Public universities are designed to cover this market failure by providing more education and basic research than the market would yield on its own; these are the fundamental roles of a university and the argument for government support'. Allowing for the historical solecism of what universities 'are designed' to do, it is nevertheless a powerful argument: an expression of the kind of hard-headed but open-minded sensibility towards universities and their sustaining society that is desperately needed if academics wish their institutions' central commitment to responsible teaching and free inquiry to survive the twenty-first century.[7]

These comments, by the American academic Steven Shapin, might well be pinned up in every British university, hopefully by the waste paper basket into which all QAA and 'Entrepreneurial Initiative' documents are being thrown. It is quite likely that this will not be the case, since British universities (and British academics) have been less energetic in the defence of the 'liberal' university than their colleagues in the United States. Because debates about higher education in Britain have been more enmeshed in debates about access (and particularly access to Oxford and Cambridge) there has been less attention to the subtle, but insidious, transformations that have been taking place in Britain. While arguments have been waging about who should go where (many arguments which take place in the United States are in the context of race rather than class), British universities have seen the gradual un-picking of the idea (not to mention the practice) that universities should *not* be at the service of the market. Unfortunately for British universities, the rhetoric about the role of the universities has been couched in the ambiguous language of the 'public good' – an idea much more difficult to resist than the straightforward adoption of the needs of commerce. It is not particularly difficult to maintain clear boundaries between work which is *explicitly* for profit and work which is not. Maintaining boundaries, when all academics are expected to interest themselves in is the entrepreneurial, for the public good, is much more difficult. Indeed, for some voices, British universities have been slow to adopt the interest of industry and commerce. To quote Shapin again:

> This July's (2003) Lambert Review of Business –University Collaboration, which slapped Cambridge's wrist for being 'slow off the mark' in technology transfer, reported British business concern that the Research Assessment Exercise – put in place as a display of management rationality disciplining feckless university culture – was now acting as an obstacle to

academic collaborations with industry: faculty, the business respondents complained, 'had much greater incentives to publish academic research than could be submitted to research assessment exercise panels than to undertake joint research with industry'.[8]

Here academics stand accused not of taking their eyes off the research ball, but of carelessly forgetting about the profit-making ball. It is probably the case that the *Lambert Review of Business–University Collaboration* is not as widely read in universities as the *Times Literary Supplement* or the *New York Review of Books* but the very fact that it exists, and exists with enough self-confidence to pontificate about the proper behaviour of academics, is less a straw in the wind than an entire haystack. Behind the sentiment voiced in the quotation lies, it is apparent, a fury that there are people in the world who have concerns other than profit; legitimated by the moral sanitization of the market economy, those committed to the market have no reservations about assuming that this is the case for everyone. But as Shapin, and other liberals in the United States such as Derek Bok, the ex-President of Harvard University, have pointed out, the commercialization of the university is actually dysfunctional in terms of both the production of valuable (in all senses) research and intellectually capable individuals. Maintaining boundaries is not just valuable for those of us who would like ten-foot walls, topped by broken glass, built between universities and the interests of profit, but also for those who have less rigid ideas about social boundaries.

In these debates, about commerce, profit, the interests of both and the universities, we can see many of those elements of other debates about modernity, capitalism and post-modernity. After 1989 and the collapse of the old Soviet Empire capitalism became the only ideological game in town for many people in the West, at the same time as the impulses of post-modernism were vastly enlarging the cultural possibilities and the nature of cultural authority in the West. On the one hand, therefore, there was a loss of one of those 'grand narratives' of the nineteenth and twentieth centuries (socialism), on the other the emergence of greater acceptance of social diversity. Yet in terms of social order, both these shifts presented problems about maintaining some form of social coherence: if the market was to run free, as was culture, from where would come the values and norms that might maintain social solidarity? The French sociologist Emile Durkheim devoted much of his life to discussing this issue, concluding that social integration is vital to both social and individual well-being. But he reached this conclusion at the beginning, rather than the end, of the twentieth century, at a time when some social certainties existed and 'grand narratives' were still intact.

The new social context, in which social integration is diminished, has been described variously as 'anomie' and 'normlessness' and has also been portrayed as the culture in which people 'bowl alone'. In his study of community life in the United States (*Bowling Alone*) Robert Putnam has called for greater general participation in social life across a range of social and political institutions. He writes:

> Nowhere is the need to restore connectedness, trust and civic engagement clearer than in the now empty public forums of our democracy ... Let us find ways to ensure that by 2010 many more Americans will participate in the public life of our communities – running for office, attending public meetings, serving on committees, campaigning in elections and even voting ... Campaign reform (above all, campaign finance reform) should be aimed at increasing the importance of social capital – and decreasing the importance of financial capital – in our elections, federal, state and local.[9]

Putnam's argument, and his exhaustively researched account of the decline of community in the United States, is driven by the decline in voting in the United States, and thus much concerned with political, as a distinct form of the civic, participation. Two comments on his study, which relate both to universities and to intellectual life, are relevant here. The first is that although Putnam emphasizes the importance of religion in the social world of the United States, what he perhaps under-plays is the receptivity of individuals in the United States to what are 'mad' (in the fullest sense) ideas. The refusal of certain school boards in the United States to allow the discussion of Charles Darwin is just one example of a society which falls victim, with some apparent ease, to the more extraordinary vagaries of fundamentalist Christianity. What is accepted at home, then becomes what is feared abroad: just as fundamentalist Christianity promotes virginity at home, so that same culture constructs pathological concern about fundamentalist elements of Islam.

In the twenty-first century it is appropriate to name, and fear, those ideas which deal only in exclusive simplicities. The traditional bulwark against simplicity, and conceptual naïvety, is education. But if education is offered only as training in repetition, then its impact and its importance in creating a population which can think independently and critically is minimized. Moreover, as Putnam points out, if that education is provided in ways which minimize social connectedness, then much of the value of that education is lost: 'In other words, at Harvard as well as in Harlem, social connectedness boosts educational attainment'.[10] Thus a society which is becoming less integrated is a society which educates less well, and is then vulnerable to becoming a society which understands less. Statistics about participation rates in higher education are, therefore, perhaps misleading in themselves and only indicative of the old adage about taking horses to water. It is clear that a lot of horses are being taken to the metaphorical water of higher education; whether or not they will, or can (as Putnam suggests) drink is another matter.

A second question that emerges from Putnam's study is the issue of the part that higher education itself is playing in speeding the decline of social connectedness. The word 'participation' is often constructed in ways which suggest that in participating, we join in and join up. It is probably no accident that the British government uses the word 'participation' to describe formal entry to higher education: 'entry' carries with it more problematic connotations, not the least of which is exit. 'Entry' also signifies a beginning, a crossing into a new place or new set of ideas. 'Participation' on the other hand suggests being part of a game, of which the rules have already been decided. There were always 'rules' in higher education for students (at various times in British, although less so in American, history to do with religious tests, dress codes and sexual access to the opposite sex) but as these rules have disappeared, new ones have taken their place about essay deadlines, attendance and formal 'participation'. The spectre of the student who attends no lectures or seminars and yet emerges with an outstanding degree in final examinations is clearly a terror to the QAA: this species has to be hunted out and identified as a highly imperfect 'participant'. Indeed, this species has now been made virtually extinct in British universities since the career of all students is marked by weekly (if not daily) demands of proof of participation. This obsessive checking has now met its real challenge: the student who attends seminars but never speaks. Is this, or is this not, participation? Anecdotal evidence indicates academic concerns; 'Miss X comes to seminars but always looks bored', 'Mr Y comes to seminars but seems shy'. Quite what is being examined here has yet to be codified by the QAA but no doubt at some point 'participation' will come to have its own check-list of facial expression, verbal fluency and body language.

It would seem, from the evidence of British universities (and evidence which is available in the various forms and elements of the so-called 'paper trail' which academics are now expected to complete, that students are now being subjected to a greater degree of surveillance than at any other time in the history of universities. Paradoxically, this is taking place at the time when students are described as 'consumers' and increasingly collecting large debts in order to acquire a university degree. Thus although students protest about debt (and top-up fees) they seldom protest about the monitoring to which they are subject, making them, as consumers, particularly passive examples of this role. The connections that could – and should – be made between the cost of a university education and the cost of providing armies of bureaucrats (the national QAA, for example, and the staff within each university essential to carrying out the QAA's *diktats*) are seldom voiced. Yet arguments about the funding of higher education need to include material about the funding necessary to support the increased bureaucratization of the sector.

The new bureaucracies of higher education include, perhaps most crucially for academics, the personnel responsible for the Research Assessment Exercise. In this exercise, we can see most clearly that destruction of social connectedness in institutions of which Robert Putnam, and others, have written. At no point in the history of universities on either side of the Atlantic (or the Channel) have academics ever been known for an outstanding ability (or wish) to form teams and alliances. Indeed, the inclination to become an academic (particularly in the social sciences and the humanities) generally involved a temperament and personality content with long periods of social isolation and highly individualized work. Competition between academics was, equally, intense, since the critique of ideas was *inter alia* the way in which careers were made. So in saying that the RAE, and other exercises, have diminished social connectedness no comparison is made here with a consensual and cooperative past in which academics eagerly exchanged ideas and helped each other on their way. Individual competition was always part and parcel of academic life and novelists (and academics themselves) have always noted the often extreme fury of academic competition. Yet what the RAE has done (and is now apparently about to take further towards individual competitiveness) is to encourage structures which quite explicitly endorse and reward competition between individuals and institutions. At present, for example, individuals are ranked in terms of 'national', 'international' and presumably inter-galactic importance; recent proposals suggest the award of stars to each academic, so that we can emerge with one, two or three stars.

In this context there is an explicit encouragement of the worst forms of exclusiveness, secrecy and divisiveness within the academy. To set up a hierarchy which labels individuals in much the same way as restaurants or hotels imposes a straitjacket of expectations and what are probably 'performance indicators'. (Were the towels clean/ does this article have sufficient footnotes?) To accept this hierarchy involves many academics in judgemental exercises about their colleagues and peers, and of course increases the opportunity for academic corruption and insider trading. Social, let alone intellectual, connectedness is hardly likely to flourish in this context as academics, academic departments and universities become locked into obsessive competitions about the award of stars. The RAE makes circus monkeys out of academics, in that it demands performance in a certain ritual of behaviour and the organization of all behaviour towards the pattern of that ritual. In societies of the West, in which social rituals are, for many people, relatively few and far in number, it would seem to be the case that institutions are developing new rituals to fill this vacuum. Thus what could be creative or innovative work (academic or otherwise, performed by staff or student) takes on ritualized forms, determined by processes external to the work itself. Perhaps most pathetic of all in the RAE is the hope that the 'new' (post-1992) universities will ever match the performance of the Russell universities; in the circus of the RAE, age and experience manifestly triumph over youth and enthusiasm.

In any discussion of the structures which have now invaded much of Western higher education, the key question that has to be answered is perhaps that of why (especially the case of Britain) governments are so determined to invade and control the academic space. It would be an exceptionally paranoid politician (in a league with Hitler and Goebbels) who actually believed, in the cold light of day, that academics could be in any way a serious threat to social stability. (When universities have been associated with social unrest, as in France in 1968, the reasons for the disruption have been largely external to the universities themselves and made visible by large numbers of young people in the same place at the same time.) Student radicalism is a fantasy of both Left and Right and has little to offer in terms of full-scale disruption. Academics themselves have sometimes been politically active, but that political activity has been as much conservative as radical and very seldom (if ever) directed towards the over-throw of governments or the de-stabilization of the state. Women and other people who make up that majority which is not white, middle class or male, have rightly protested about the exclusiveness of universities, but that protest has been directed towards inclusion rather than restructuring. It is difficult to find, in the history of any university anywhere in the Western world, evidence of behaviour or intent which presents the possibility of real social disruption.

We therefore have to look further than universities themselves for the reasons why the state (and indeed often universities themselves) have become so hopelessly enthusiastic about the control of the process of thinking and teaching. What, indeed, is the fear that drives people towards the QAA? Can it be that a generation has emerged which having assiduously put its record collection into alphabetical order now wishes to impose the same order on the academy? As Paul Newman said (of the people pursuing him) to Robert Redford in the film *Butch Cassidy and the Sundance Kid*, 'who *are* these people?' The men and women who are nationally described as 'the suits' have emerged from the same social world as their detractors; can we detect in the behaviour of the bureaucrats of higher education a fear of spontaneity and, indeed, an absence of its experience. The disappearance of widespread economic scarcity and the ending of explicit sexual repression in the West allowed us to live apparently more prosperous and autonomous lives than our parents and grandparents. But at the same time other ideas about the fears of terrorism, personal attack and risks in everyday life became part of the general culture. The 'modern' world which emerged at the beginning of the twentieth century coincided with the sinking of the Titanic; the very emblem of modern, technological achievement failed to achieve what the Vikings had managed ten centuries before: the safe crossing of the northern Atlantic. So we began to insure, not just for the one event we can all expect – our own funerals – but against fire, against burglary, against, most recently, growing sexually unattractive. The paradox of the modern world is therefore that just as, for many people in the West, the world becomes more objectively predictable, the subjective experience of that world is that it is more unreliable and unstable.

The mind-set which produced the QAA is not one which is all that pleasant to consider, since its chief elements appear to be a desire for the punishment of others far greater than anything Foucault encountered when writing *Discipline and Punish*, that great account of the birth of disciplinary institutions.[11] The QAA is precisely that, an institution set upon bringing a world into line with its expectations, expectations which in its case are narrow-minded, fearful, prosaic and entirely uneducated. As a model of what education is about the QAA stands with those individuals (and institutions) so savagely parodied in the eighteenth century: the narrow-minded clerics of Henry Fielding's *Tom Jones* and the definition of education provided by the Bertram sisters in Jane Austen's *Mansfield Park*. Austen and Fielding both knew that education could be reduced to nothing except the observance of form: in *Emma*, Austen wrote of those schools which did little for their pupils except impart jargon:

> Mrs Goddard was the mistress of a School – not of a seminary, or an establishment, or anything which professed, in long sentences of refined

nonsense, to combine liberal acquirements with elegant morality upon new principles and new systems – and where young ladies for enormous pay might be screwed out of health and into vanity.[12]

The 'enormous pay' necessary to support the experience of higher education has now become a reality in Britain; for it, what many students receive is a familiarity with the processing of information – collect the hand-out, reproduce it and there is the necessary, quantifiable achievement. It is a form of attendance ritual which is legitimated by the twenty-first century's equivalent of 'liberal acquirements', the idea that a society becomes more 'equal' because half of an age group have taken part in our contemporary version of the 'seminary' which Austen parodies. The demands of the QAA and the RAE are both a daily nuisance and, more seriously, a divisive presence in the university (in that a new form of confrontation, of assessors and assessed, is introduced where none previously existed) but although this is unfortunate for academics, the most important consequence of these developments is the gradual reversal of liberal ideas about education and the disappearance of the acceptance of the *implicit* risks, inconsistencies and ambiguities of education at its very best. The finest education is one without aims and objectives; it is not directed towards social norms, or forms.

The terror of the modern was, in the first part of

the twentieth century, all too evident in those
fascist states which embraced a mythical version of
their own past. The modern, with its toleration of
the emancipation of women, the encouragement
of the understanding of the human psyche and the
establishment of democratic institutions, was
deeply disturbing to patriarchical hierarchies,
both material and symbolic. The partial accom-
modation achieved between modernity and tradition was then intensified by the demands of post-
modernism, demands that included not just the
re-examination of certain social categories but
their dissolution and disappearance. Rank, gender, race and age all become disposable divisions.
Little wonder that the possible conceptual anar-
chy of this world was deeply problematic to some
of those concerned with examination and assessment: how, in this new world, were distinctions
and differences to be made?

These real intellectual issues, of what and how
we judge, were overtaken before they could be
considered by the demands of the state for a system
of higher education which seemed to be 'equal',
'modern', and effective. A public schooled in
consumerist expectations about access to goods
and services would not tolerate apparently élitist
divisions and expectations, and thus institutional
re-labelling made possible a more general award of
degrees and entry to 'university'. Legitimating this
experience (and the amount of money individuals
had to contribute to take part in it) demanded
some national, apparently egalitarian systems other
than the self-policing which had always existed in

universities. The 'dogs of war' which were let loose in this process were ancient jealousies between the privileged and the less so, between those who had benefited more than those who had benefited less. The eager recruits to law and order who have made possible every fascist regime in history found a civilian, and respectable, place for themselves in the QAA and its endorsing institutions. If 'every woman adores a fascist' then every university seemed to contain at least enough people willing to learn to live to control others through new patterns of surveillance.

The sentence 'every woman loves a fascist' was written by Sylvia Plath and is a line in what is probably one of her most famous poems, 'Daddy'.[13] The poem makes connections between the Holocaust and her own recollections of her father which have been widely discussed and analysed elsewhere.[14] Here, what is relevant is the way in which Plath's rage emerged out of a number of her own experiences, one of which was her mother's suppression of her own feeling and inclinations. In a chilling account of the early days of her own marriage Mrs Aurelia Plath wrote:

> (Otto) had never known the free flow of communication that characterized my relationship with my family, and talking things out and reasoning together just didn't operate. At the end of our first year of marriage, I realized that if I wanted a peaceful home – and I did – I would simply have to become more submissive, although it was not my nature to be so.[15]

This account of the curtailment of the spirit is of an individual case, but it is possible to see the processes and structures of contemporary higher education as of a similar kind, and derived from a similar source – the fear of the loss of power and authority by the powerful. The result is hardly likely to be the intense fury which Sylvia Plath expressed of the man who stood at the blackboard ('You stand at the blackboard, daddy') but what informed the world (of both Sylvia Plath and her mother) was a sense of education as both deeply desirable and yet also a form of control. Even more so, one of the unities between Sylvia Plath and Ted Hughes was their shared suspicion of the academic order – an academic order which when they experienced it in the 1950s was entirely anarchic by today's standards. Watching his wife prepare to teach at Smith College, Ted Hughes wrote of 'the misery of your blue flannel suit', a comment as much about the complex relationship between universities and creativity as it was about Sylvia Plath's ambivalence to university education.[16]

For over two hundred years there has been a contest in Western culture between the romantic and the rational, and no doubt many advocates of the *status quo* in contemporary universities would interpret the above as evidence of a displaced romanticism about higher education. Implicitly, these critics would assume that they occupy the sacred space of the 'rational', little aware that the only space which they clearly occupy is that of the servants of the rationality of the market economy – and indeed probably not even that. There is little that is 'rational', in the sense of critical thought, about the QAA and a great deal that is actually both irrational and socially dysfunctional. The endorsement and encouragement (indeed the explicit expectation) of individual and institutional competition, the intolerance of difference and diversity both decreases social cohesion and the quality of education itself. The 'sleep of reason' has always been assumed to be the triumph of fools and knaves as much as the birth of monsters: nowhere could this prediction be more true than in contemporary universities. In profoundly conservative and socially timorous ways, the bureaucrats of higher education turn their backs on the intellectual possibilities of late modernity and the post-modern world and seek refuge in the authoritarian enclaves of conceptual worlds which are mean, divisive and parochial. In this they reverse many of the conditions of intellectual creativity in the past, in which great works of the imagination were achieved within narrow, and limited confines. As the material and social world has become wider and more tolerant, the ranks of the academic police have attempted to curb the imaginative possibilities of this world. The paradox of contemporary universities is therefore that as the world becomes larger, the academic space becomes smaller and more narrowly confined.

# Survival Strategies

Writing has always been part of a survival strategy for those at odds with the public realm, since it has allowed individuals to occupy both a conventional private space while constructing a radical world of the imagination. Charlotte Brontë and Jane Austen are just two examples of the women who remained entirely dutiful at the same time as they were writing works of radical challenge. Writing is not just about the conscientious fulfilment of professional expectations; it can also be about protest. Hopefully, this account of contemporary British universities is part of that tradition, and as such an attempt to externalize some of the misery and the isolation which can too often be the lot of the academic. Academic work might appear to take place in contexts which involve cooperation and social contact, but much of that cooperation and contact is tinged with the competition of professional institutional life. There is discussion, and there are meetings, but one of the core functions of the academic – to write for publication – takes place in the lonely privacy of the office and the study. It is not, of course, that academics generally deplore the opportunity to be alone with a pen, or a word processor, but what is taken to that private place is often the nagging and remorseless imperatives of an assessment-driven culture. Most academics went into university teaching because they felt that they had something to say, in either print or in person. So few academics were actually unwilling to publish. Apart from those who are unfortunately word blocked and who cannot put pen to paper, most academics regarded (and regard) a blank sheet of paper/empty computer screen as a challenge to our competence.

It is not, therefore, that academics have ever been forced to write; on the contrary, most of us talk longingly of 'time to write' and apply for research grants so that we can spend more time writing. We willingly sign up for that lonely, isolated time in which we pitch our wits against the assembled knowledge in our subject and attempt to demonstrate our erudition, our formidable intelligence and the originality of our arguments. Alone with our pens and our keyboards we embody the wagers of both Protestantism and Roman Catholicism: we take a chance that our endeavours will save us, make us immortal and prove us correct in choosing our calling; we take a chance that God exists, and that in some way God will admit us to heaven. Both strands of Christianity formidably coincide in the academic exercise of writing: we have saints to appeal to for help (those other colleagues, those networks which might intervene to help us) but at the same time the ultimate responsibility for our destiny is our own.

The confidence and the determination to embark on the life of the academic thus requires – if the academic mark is to be made – iron will and a stubborn, sometimes blind, belief that what we, individually, have to say is worth saying. In certain contexts in the past, there were certainly well-rewarded academics who wrote very little, or who were regarded as great thinkers through the sharpness of their wits or their conformity to certain patrician views of originality. The context in which this construction of the worth while being academic was to be found was largely that of Oxbridge, described by Terry Eagleton thus:

> If a don spits in your beef stew or allows his pet parrot to lacerate your cheekbone, he is simply being loveably idiosyncratic. Many old-style academics have preferred to be thought colourful rather than honest. Their aim is to be fine, not good. Eccentricity, a fancy word for outrageous egoism, was to traditional Oxbridge what normality is to police sergeants. The homosexual John Sparrow opposed homosexual law reform on the grounds that it would take the spice out of being gay. A disgusting old misogynist who derived a positively erotic frisson from resisting enlightened reform, this malicious, supremely trivial-minded warden of All Souls (or All Holes, as the college became known after he gleefully spotted a passage about buggery in D.H. Lawrence) had no interest in ideas, chalked up no academic or

other achievements worth nothing, and thought it amusing to joke about killing babies.[1]

This is inspired rhetoric about a particular place (and person) at a particular time. Whether or not this culture of ultimately timorous and certainly tedious prejudice was the only culture of Oxbridge is debatable, as is the question of whether or not the small-minded, intellectual incompetence of John Sparrow *et al.* actually mattered. All Souls might have been over-privileged in various material ways, but it could equally well have been a somewhat pathetic cultural backwater.

For many British academics who were educated in the 1960s and the 1970s there will have been encounters with both the real thing of the worst idiocies of Oxbridge culture and its imitators in other universities. The allure of complete and absolute privilege was always seductive to some, just as there was furious antagonism against it by others. The problem of the culture of Oxbridge was not, however, the degree of its idiocy, but the dilemma of its often considerable brilliance, particularly in those subjects (the natural sciences and mathematics) where the practioners were less likely to make judgements that were exclusively, rather than partially, subjective. Assessing an individual's standing in the 'culture stakes' was, and is, more difficult than assessing their abilities to understand and contribute to scientific and mathematical knowledge. We know that Oxford did not think much of Margaret Thatcher and we know that Rosalind Franklin encountered difficulties in her social relations with male colleagues in the laboratory, but these two judgements suggest the range of misogyny at Oxbridge.[2] Yet traditional institutions, replete as Oxbridge was with vicious, self-seeking, plain daft old men, were not necessarily always wrong and it was certainly not an intellectual wasteland. Within this traditional world, and within the red-brick civic universities of the 1960s, academics were often free to teach and publish as they wished.

It was the case, in these years, that expertise at teaching was certainly not rewarded in any monetary sense, but nor was publishing the absolute *sine qua non* of academic life. Academics did publish, in the same way as some did have higher degrees, and particularly so in the natural sciences. But there was no absolute requirement that academics had to have either higher degrees or a list of publications on their *curriculum vitae*. When David Lodge wrote *Changing Places* in 1975 he contrasts the British academic Philip Swallow with the energetic writer Morris Zapp. (It is clear that the writer's sympathies are mixed: Swallow is careful and well read about his subject, but hesitant to commit himself on paper; Zapp is prolific in his publications, but perhaps over zealous in this very energy.)[3] These are stereotypes of academics from the United States and Britain, but stereotypes which are not impossibly far from the reality of universities in the 1970s. Writing in these days was possible, but not necessary, for British academics.

Suddenly, however, it seemed as if the flood gates had opened on the arid lands of British academic publication. New universities, new audiences and new forms of competition created a new ecology in the universities: publication was everywhere, and it became, after the first British Research Assessment Exercise (RAE), a matter of first necessity and then compulsion that academics should write. Stakhanov had arrived from Stalin's Russia in the British academy, and with him – or his reincarnation – came the demand that every academic in the land should, over a five-year period, produce four pieces of written work. As Assessment Exercises went on, the rules about what counted, and what did not count, changed: increasingly only publications in certain journals 'mattered' – just as some publishing houses 'mattered' more than others. The term 'presti-gious journal' was bandied about to impress upon would-be authors that their offerings only 'really' counted if they were released to the world in those 'rigorously peer reviewed' journals which became the sacred place of assessors.

The enthusiasm for publication thus created in the British academy could not, in these circum-stances, be described as the blooming of the desert or the Renaissance of the British campus. Both these terms suggest the natural or the accidental, whereas the reality was more like factory farming. As always had been the case, much was published which was valuable, interesting and genuinely relevant to the subject in question. Equally, the created pressure to publish marginalized and excluded those who did not wish to write, or write very often, and encouraged a new set of bureaucratic structures to distinguish between forms and locations of publication. Pinning your thoughts on a church door was, in this culture, not acceptable. Never mind that those thoughts might transform the cultural map of Europe; Martin Luther's intellectual engagement, like that of Einstein or Wittgenstein, would not have met the criteria of the RAE. The quota demanded by the Stakhanovite regime now at work in universities defeats some, just as it is nothing to those with fluency on paper. As Stakhanov himself demonstrated, what is shown by the imposition of quotas is not just how much can be produced under the optimum circumstances (as was the case in Stakhanov's own achievement) but how little is achieved by the rest. So the quota of four publications, now demanded of every academic who does not wish to acquire the dreaded label of 'research inactive' is not, to some people, very much. The point is not the extent of the quota, but that the quota is there at all and that through it an activity which was previously optional and voluntary has been made compulsory. Whereas once writing and publishing might have been the form of resistance to a culture of amateurism and the narrow standards of a particular university, now *not* writing could be a form of resistance to an equally provincial set of standards and an entirely mechanistic assessment of academic value.

A good deal is made in RAEs of the idea of assessment of academics by their 'peers', an idea which is clearly part of the legitimation of the whole exercise. But anyone who has been an academic for any length of time comes to recognize that academics, like all other professions, have hierarchies of importance and influence. In part, it is the essential function of professions to maintain these hierarchies and it is equally part of the long-term impact of Thatcherism that 'professional' (in the sense of specialist and not market-driven) expertise was forced to take second place to the ideologues of the free market. Yet professions, while entirely defensible in their defence of their own understanding and specialist knowledge, can become corrupt when their interests are threatened. Academics do not, on the whole, accept large bribes, but they are just as likely to work towards the maintenance of the *status quo* as any other group whose interests are threatened. So it has been with the RAE: in subtle and often unremarked ways the rules of engagement have been allowed to reflect the interests of the already powerful, while 'insider trading' has often allowed the fine print of the exercise to be written by those who are well aware of how to benefit themselves, or their institutions. The shifts, compromises and agreements are complex, many and varied, but the results of the RAE are not; unto those that have shall be given, and if you have not, do not even consider the possibility of gain.

The confirmation of the universities of Oxford, Cambridge and London as the major victors of the RAE demonstrates the vitality of those often attacked citadels of high culture and privilege. Much as the post-1992 universities may have initially supported the Exercise, the hoped for democratization of funding has failed to materialize. Indeed, what has occurred is that research funding is even less democratically distributed than in the past, where many 'old' universities operated on a playing field which was more or less equal. Now the emergence of an élite group within 'old' universities further brutalizes the whole culture of universities: there is no democracy in a system which separates colleague from colleague, department from department and sets up fierce competition both within and between institutions. All this, it has to be remembered, takes place in institutions which were never strangers to competition and rivalry. Imposing more competition on a system which was already competitive suggests either a fanciful view of the positive impact of competition on human activity or a cynical understanding of the chances of anyone except the most powerful and the best funded doing well in academic contests.

Of these two possibilities, the first – the idea that competition actually encourages better teaching, more creative research and stimulating publication – was for some academics part of the seductive fantasies of the Thatcher era. Class divisions, antagonisms and rivalries being what they are in British universities it was probably inevitable that post-1992 universities would see an opportunity in the new world of competitive higher education to oust the most powerful from their places. Mrs Thatcher effectively sold a particular view of the positive impact of competition to many middle-class professionals, since she seemed to offer a sense of empowerment which was being eroded by the demands of mass higher education. The mantras of the 1980s in universities included 'control of the budget', 'departmental business plans' and 'income streams'. These new responsibilities appeared to give academics (or some academics) more independence and a more properly integrated role in the funding of universities. In point of fact it gave most academics who took on these responsibilities no such thing: people whose specialist subjects were Augustan poetry or molecular biology found themselves confronted by demands for business plans and evidence of entrepreneurship. Let other pens dwell on the human misery that these demands produced: the essential point was that the shift in the extension and re-definition of academic responsibilities was pointlessly ideological and, in the fullest sense, irrational. There was no sensible reason, in terms of the nurturance and development of universities, to ask academics to become very partly skilled, and entirely untrained accountants.

The strength of Thatcherism was that it could not imagine individuals (or institutions) which existed independent of the cash nexus. 'Strength' is used deliberately here because the narrow-minded lack of imagination of Thatcherism was, indeed, both Thatcherism's greatest strength and its greatest weakness. The strength lay in the resonance which Thatcherism had for a very mixed group of the British population, a group which encompassed both international corporations (which initially saw in Thatcherism freedom from workplace controls and lower rates of taxation) and workers and small-business owners (who imagined a world in which they would become truly independent). For both groups the fantasy failed to be realized: social unrest and an under-funded infrastructure were too high a price to pay for illusory, or non-existent, gains. Yet what remained, and to a significant extent still remains in all complex, Western capitalist societies, is the belief that competition between individuals and institutions is a socially necessary healthy tension. It has proved difficult, though not impossible, to make schools and hospitals competitive in the sense of direct engagement with the economy. There is, despite the explicit and the latent Thatcherism of the past twenty years, a sense in which the core function of schools and hospitals is difficult to bring entirely into a close relationship with the values of the market economy. Successive governments have introduced, and endlessly refined, league tables between schools and hospitals, but these tables usually bear some relationship to either education or healing the sick.

Universities were always an easier target for those who wished to bend all public institutions to the will of the market. First, many civic/red-brick universities had long traditions of engagement with local industries and often provided training which was explicitly about the needs of the local economy. Second, universities have often shown themselves willing to accept funding from private individuals or private industries, albeit occasionally in ways which have resulted in controversy. Third, the links (both social and ideological) between certain universities and the powerful have always been close; for many generations much of Britain's mandarin class was Oxbridge educated and accustomed to the view that these universities were a core part of the nature of the state. Nevertheless, what Mrs Thatcher entirely underestimated (an underestimation which resulted in her symbolic rejection by the University of Oxford) was the degree to which élite universities did not take kindly to threats to their independence and autonomy.

As Tony Blair's government was also to discover, the belief that universities could be turned to the will and the service of the State (in the case of the Blair government the question of the extension in the number of state school pupils admitted to Oxbridge) was deeply resisted. For liberals, just as much as conservatives, universities are both an easier but a more complex target: easy because they have a history of cooperation with the world outside their walls, but more complex because they are often willing to defend areas of independence. It is unfortunate, therefore, that universities have refused to resist the competition imposed upon them by measures such as the RAE. The Exercise (which began as an attempt to distribute funding for the expensive natural sciences) has arguably little merit for students and teachers other than to distort research and exaggerate the possibilities of academic authoritarianism. For example, at present the Office of Science and Technology has put forward proposals that in effect will make it impossible for anyone in a university which does not have critical proportions of 'world class' research to develop further research.[4] For élite universities this means that more of the available cake is going to go in their direction; for others it means that individuals in poorly rated universities will have little or no chance of applying for research: the ship sinks and so does everyone else on it. The Office of Science and Technology assumes, of course, that the RAE is faultless at identifying excellence in research, despite the very obvious problem that the RAE by definition looks backward rather than forward. Despite the pious verbiage produced in RAE submissions which promise 'further developments', 'ongoing research' and more trajectories than there are legs on a centipede, RAE assessors can only assess what has already been produced. Differences have been observed between the 1995 and the 2001 RAEs; despite the fact that fewer researchers were submitted in 2001, almost a quarter of them moved from departments with a grade of one to four to departments with a grade of five or five star.[5] What we can deduce from this (besides the fact that the 1995 exercise could not accurately predict how good researchers might become) is that, first, universities became more skilled at assembling winning teams and, second, that at least some academics on at least some subject panels experienced a surge of fellow feeling and were more generous in their assessments.

To this revival of the spirit of the solidarity of labour the government responded by refusing, in the case of England and Wales, to give research funding to departments graded at four or less. The message was clear: don't try and get subversive with us; we have ways of making sure that funding is distributed in ways which we – the government – want and not otherwise. Thus departments which had received an entirely reputable grade, albeit in a disreputable exercise, were left unfunded for research and at the mercy of any university administrator who wished to use the opportunity to impose sanctions on staff. The financial costs of not being research funded matter, and matter considerably, but it is also worth remembering the psychic costs to the people involved. To be removed from the charmed circle of 'research funded' inevitably brings with it a sense of failure and exclusion, but a sense which is complicated by questions of responsibility for that failure. Individuals may very well value their own work, and receive praise for it: but that value comes to nothing if the work of others is of neglible importance. An extraordinary relationship is thus produced between academics: members of a profession which is about the demonstration of individuated ideas are forced into dependence on immediate others. The collective is assessed and hence, however talented the individual is, it is through the collective that salvation is achieved or lost. Even though the present proposals about the next RAE suggest a star system (one star for a member of the academic *corps de ballet* to three stars for the *prima ballerina*) no individual is going to be allowed to pocket the money and run – which would, of course, be the logical outcome of the proposals for a highly individualized system.

We are, as academics in contemporary Britain, increasingly set against each other. If not actually set at each other's throats we are nevertheless encouraged (indeed dragooned) into participating in a culture in which the level of competition might make the ordinary free marketer flinch. Many 'modern' practices of management stress the importance of encouraging cooperation and consensus in the workplace; it is perceived as rational to ensure that people who work together can actually assist each other in the shared enterprise. The latest proposals for the evaluation of academics, the 'star' system proposed by the Roberts recommendation, emphasizes the individual rather than the group in a way which certainly reflects the highly individual way in which many academics in the humanities and social sciences might wish to work, but does little to support the mutual enterprise in which academics are involved which is that of teaching. Indeed, the new rationality for academics post-Roberts would be, and no doubt will be, the pursuit of entirely ruthless individualism. Being awarded those three stars guarantees an envied place in the academic market, an irrefutable status in the professional world; until the next Assessment Exercise the award of all those stars confers the apparent right to assume that one has reached the pinnacle of academic achievement.

The problem of this new form of academic assessment is that it enfolds academics within the judgement of their peers and creates inside the academy endless opportunities for corruption, personal vendettas and the kind of nit-picking behaviour which has always been a part of academic practice. Every member of every assessment panel now has an opportunity to settle those old scores, to take revenge on the bad review, the sarcastic remarks, the casual viciousness and the professional rivalry of the past. It is a new and singularly exclusive way of ensuring that a pyramid is produced within British universities: the present winners will win again and their rewards will be even greater as the degree of differentiation between universities increases. English – rather more than British – higher education is very much involved in the reproduction of a certain culture of privilege; not a simple reproduction of social privilege (although this also occurs) but the reproduction of a certain attitude to the world, and to knowledge. In *Three Guineas* Virginia Woolf took a sceptical view of the merits of education which remains relevant:

> Need we collect more facts from history and biography to prove our statement that all attempt to influence the young against war through the education they receive at the

universities must be abandoned? For do they not prove that education, the finest education in the world, does not teach people to hate force, but to use it? Do they not prove that education, far from teaching the educated generosity and magnanimity, makes them on the contrary so anxious to keep their possessions, that 'grandeur and power' of which the poet speaks, in their own hands, that they will use not force but much subtler methods than force when asked to share them?[6]

The questions which Woolf asks, and the critical view which she takes of the value of education, would now no doubt be regarded as heretical in many quarters. Questioning the value of higher education would be seen as akin to questioning the value of democracy or the value of 'healthy' eating. Certain kinds of values about 'how to live' have become part of the taken-for-granted rhetoric of the twenty-first century and part of the rhetoric is the belief that higher education is, *ipso facto*, a 'good' thing. Yet, as Woolf recognized, participation in (and accreditation through) higher education does not necessarily produce more democratic, more generous or even more open-minded people. It is as likely to produce individuals who have a sense of their own value and the legitimate rewards that are theirs, legitimate because they have participated in a world of privilege. The cut throat competition which now faces would-be entrants to the universities of Oxford, Cambridge and London is no longer just about a social élite being educated at 'their' universities, it is about a political and cultural élite (many of whose members may well be drawn from a social élite) recognizing that only entry to these élite institutions will offer them a reassuringly significant opportunity of locating themselves in the dominant culture. That culture is, certainly, pluralistic and diverse, but it is about, as Woolf knew, the 'grandeur' of power.

In contemporary Britain, there is a strong case for the argument that cultural divisions are becoming more distinct, and more closely linked to the distribution of social and economic power than at any time in the history of the past one hundred years. Culture, as a number of sociologists (including A. H. Halsey and Pierre Bourdieu) have reminded us, is a commodity, and a valuable one at that.[7] It is a commodity which we can, of course, be born with access to, in that we may (or may not) be born into families with a fluency in that most basic element of culture – language. All families talk, but some talk (and write and read) more than others, and more often in ways which under-pin access to the written word. That access is, of course, crucial for educational success in all subjects, if most particularly in the humanities and the social sciences. To be born with a ready access to the idea, not just of education, but of the possibilities of words and meanings, allows an easier access to those 'markers' of European high culture such as a classic literary tradition and works of philosophy.

Even if it is allowed that the English school curriculum has been extended to include works outside the traditional boundaries of high culture it remains the case that the discussion of these works involves, if it is successful, a facility with words and meaning.

There is a strong case, given the above, for arguing that élite higher education in England has become more the preserve of a cultural élite than a social élite. The élite universities still admit extraordinary numbers of pupils from public schools, but aside from that relatively small number of places at Oxbridge actually reserved for public school children, those pupils now have to take part in an intensely competitive process of demonstrating cultural facility. It is, as state schools have realized, a facility that can be learned and acquired, and learning it offers a way through those sacred portals of Oxford and Cambridge. The social 'snootiness' and exclusivity which were once the hallmark of many Oxbridge admissions exercises now appear closer to cultural evaluation, and the evaluation that is going on assesses qualities that are most often acquired in the home rather than the school. The great resource, the unchallengeable strength of this exercise, is that 'culture' is a truly slippery beast: the child with the exceptional exam results can be damned because she or he 'smacks too much of the midnight oil; the child with the less than outstanding exam results can be admitted because he or she thinks 'originally'. The meaning of these judgements is endlessly unclear:

thinking 'originally' may involve nothing more
than a bizarre cultural reference; outstanding
exam results may well indicate outstanding
ability.

Culture, in the twenty-first century, could
therefore be advanced as both the great new form
of social power and at the same time the continued
mask of crude social and economic power. Gay
power, black power and grey power are all forms,
and examples, of cultural resistance to an otherwise hegemonic culture and all have led to certain
accommodations within that culture. Culture, in
the sense of the visibly public, and the publicly
available, has, in the past thirty years, become
more pluralistic. This new 'diversity' is widely
presented as liberating and positive, yet what it
accompanies is a form of higher education which,
in explicitly encouraging a pyramid-shaped hierarchy, creates a bounded and restricted cultural
world. It is a great paradox of the late twentieth
and early twenty-first centuries that the democratization of culture has been accompanied by the
greater social power (and by implication the
greater material rewards) of an élite culture. That
élite culture is no longer about familiarity with
certain pinnacles of cultural achievement
(although that remains important) but it is about
the ability to demonstrate cultural literacy and
understanding. In another context (that of a
discussion of the ways in which 'the feminine' is
valued and valuable) both Beverley Skeggs and
Linda McDowell have written about the 'value' of
femininity.[8] For example, Beverley Skeggs has

suggested that working-class women acquire a particular form of femininity because it has an economic and a social value. But, and it is a very important but, defining femininity is not made autonomously by women themselves; it is made within a set of social relationships in which women are less powerful than men and endlessly subject to the constraints of masculine demand. So it may well be with 'culture' and the label 'cultured'; the people who wish to maintain social privilege and social hierarchy can define what this means, and through this control entry to those élite institutions which predictably allow greater access to social privilege. In short, the powerful control the goal posts; however much the game of culture seems to become more and more inclusive, it is nevertheless a game in which the socially powerful control the rules of the game. The government of Britain might very well achieve its aim of persuading fifty per cent of the age cohort onto the playing field of higher education, but those who are going to score on that playing field are likely to remain a select number.

Higher education in Britain thus proceeds in a curious way at the beginning of the twenty-first century. More people are allowed access to higher education than ever before, but the most valuable rewards of higher education are, arguably, more concentrated (and at least as exclusive) as in the past. At the same time, higher education has become part of a ruthlessly calculative culture. In an essay, 'The Economy of Symbolic Goods', Bourdieu has argued:

The spirit of calculation which was constantly repressed is progressively asserted as the conditions favourable to its exercise and its public affirmation are developed. The emergence of the economic field marks the appearance of a universe in which social agents can admit to themselves and admit publicly that they have interests and can tear themselves away from collective misrecognition; a universe in which they not only can do business, but can also admit to themselves that they are there to do business, that is, to conduct themselves in a self-interested manner, to calculate, make a profit, accumulate, exploit.[9]

The quotation describes vividly the world of British universities in the twenty-first century. The universities did not fight, or even resist with any great willpower, the determination of Mrs Thatcher and her government to impose the values of the market economy on every public institution and as a consequence of that lack of resistance they are endlessly subject to pressures to become more clearly the tools of the State. Anyone who has worked in universities in the past twenty years will have experienced the feral, atavistic and essentially brutal competition unleashed upon and between academics. At the same time, groups of academics (in ships which are less likely to sink than some others) have banded together to use their own existing exclusivity in ways which further separate them from others.

In summary, the present woes of higher education can be listed as fourfold: the brutalization of the culture of the academy through assessment and appraisal exercises, the creation of further hierarchy and division between universities where none needs exist, the intensification of social difference through the 'culture wars' of the universities and finally, although hardly least, the overall diminution of the essential function of the universities which is to educate, and not to train. This last proposition may appear to be just a matter of words, but it is an issue where the words do matter, and where the words are everything. If academics do not defend the importance of words (and the importance of education rather than training) then we have little right to occupy that space. Unless we wish to live in a world where difference, nuance, boundaries and indeed disagreement disappear into the iron grip of the bureaucracy of the market economy we have a responsibility to demonstrate our engagement (and interest in) the context within which we work. The temptation to disappear into our own private spaces is, for many academics, a very powerful one, but we might consider, occasionally, the rewards of occupying a more collective space. Debate, discussion and even disruption do provide interest and inspiration and it is often the less well-ordered context which gives rise to the more creative work. Efficiency in, let us say, public transport, is not the same as efficiency in the universities. If these august institutions are not to become empty parodies of their former selves we might wish to recover some of the rich possibilities of academic disorder.

The title of this book suggested the possibility of a death in the ivory tower of the university. There is little or no chance that the towers of the university (ivory or otherwise) will collapse and tumble: the walls of the universities are, in the twenty-first century, far too well protected to run the risk of collapse. But there is a chance that the towers will slowly empty of creative engagement and creativity, as new generations, having experienced the deadly possibilities of the bureaucratized university, refuse to consider further involvement with that world and take their energies and their talents elsewhere. If that occurs, then perhaps universities as we once knew them have run their course. Perhaps the real democratization of the universities will lie in the departure of future generations from them; it may be the case that ideas no longer need to be contained in a particular space. If so, we might consider the liberating possibilities of this idea rather than continuing to bring about change by the punishing rituals of the contemporary university. If we are going to develop education in new ways, we might consider doing so in ways which do the least damage to those most concerned with it. Escaping from the new punishment of education demands a public will, but hardly impossible once we recognize that we have also escaped from previous punishments of, for example, rote learning and gross social exclusiveness. Above all, if education is to mean anything in liberal democracy we need to recognize that it is not necessary to equate it with conformity and punishing regimes of assessment. We could, at the beginning of the twenty-first century, take the chance on the rewards of a genuine academic freedom.

# Notes

*Through the Looking Glass: or what Pierre Bourdieu and Kingsley Amis have in common*

1. Kingsley Amis, *Lucky Jim* (Harmondsworth, Penguin, 1954), p. 15
2. *Lucky Jim*, p. 277
3. Richard Hoggart, *The Uses of Literacy* (Harmondsworth, Penguin, 1957), pp. 169–201
4. Pierre Bourdieu, *Practical Reason* (Cambridge, Polity, 1998), p. 47
5. *Lucky Jim*, p. 24
6. Christopher Caudwell, *Studies in a Dying Culture* (New York, Monthly Review Press, 1974); Virginia Woolf, *Three Guineas* (Oxford, Oxford University Press, 1992)
7. Committee on Higher Education, *Higher Education* (The Robbins Report), Cmnd. 2154 (London, HMSO, 1963), p. 8
8. Robbins Report, p. 15
9. David Morgan and Linda McDowell, *Patterns of Residence* (Guildford, Society for Research into Higher Education, 1979), p. 12
10. See the discussion in Janet Batsleer, Tony Davies, Rebecca O'Rourke and Chris Weedon

(eds), *Rewriting English: Cultural Politics of Gender and Class* (London, Methuen, 1985)

11. Philip Larkin, 'When the Russian tanks roll westward', *Collected Poems* (London, Faber and Faber, 1988), p. 172

12. Terry Eagleton, *The Idea of Culture* (Oxford, Blackwell, 2000), p. 51

13. Philip Larkin, 'Posterity', *Collected Poems*, p. 170

14. Marilyn Strathern, '"Improving ratings": audit in the British university system', *European Review*, Vol. 5, No. 3, 1997, pp. 305–21, p. 307

15. Jarrett Report, *Report of the Steering Committee for Efficiency Studies in Universities* (London, CVCP, 1985); Dearing Report, UK National Committee of Inquiry into Higher Education: Higher Education in the Learning Society: Summary Report (London, HMSO, 1997). For a critique of Dearing please see Nicholas Barr and Iain Crawford, 'The Dearing Report and the Government's Response: A Critique', *Political Quarterly*, Vol. 69, No. 1, 1998, pp. 72–84.

16. Theodore Adorno, *Minima Moralia* (London, Verso, 1974), p. 113

17. Theodor Adorno, *Minima Moralia* (London, NLB, 1974), p. 135

18. Kingsley Amis, *Jake's Thing* (Harmondsworth, Penguin, 1987), p. 113

19. Pierre Bourdieu, *Practical Reason*, p. 128

## *The Heart of Darkness: Audit and Compliance*

1. Michael Burleigh, 'Assessment', *Times Higher Education Supplement*, 4 April 2003, p. 12

2. Alison Wolf, *Times Higher Education Supplement*, 4 April 2003, p. 13

3. Tony Mooney, 'Time's up for Ofsted', *Guardian Education*, 8 July 2003, p. 2; I. Shaw, D. P. Newton, M. Aitken and R. Darnell, 'Do Ofsted inspections of secondary schools make a difference to GCSE results?', *British Educational Research Journal*, Vol. 29, No. 1, January 2003, pp. 2–20

4. Orlando Figes, *A People's Tragedy* (London, Pimlico, 1996)

5. Joseph Stalin, 'An End to Specialist-Baiting', in Martin McCanley, *Stalin and Stalinism* (Harlow, Pearson, 1999), p. 93

6. Max Weber, *On Charisma and Institution Building* (Chicago, University of Chicago Press, 1968), p. 28

7. Zygmunt Bauman, *Modernity and the Holocaust* (Cambridge, Polity, 1991)

8. Theodor Adorno, Betty Aron, Maria Hertz Levinson and William Morrow; *The Authoritarian Personality* (New York, John Wiley, 1964) Michael Burleigh, *The Third Reich: A New History* (London, Macmillan, 2000)

9. George Eliot, *Middlemarch* (London, Everyman's Library, 1930)

10. E. P. Thompson, *Warwick University Ltd* (Harmondsworth, Penguin, 1970), p. 154

11. Michael Innes, *Death at the President's Lodging* (Harmondsworth, Penguin, 1958); Dorothy Sayers, *Gaudy Night* (London, Fontana, 1982); Carolyn Heilbrun (writing as Amanda Cross), *Death in a Tenured Position* (London, Virago, 1980)

12. George Monbiot, *Captive State* (London, Macmillan, 2000)
13. Charles Clarke, quoted in the *Times Higher Education Supplement*, 16 May 2003, p. 3
14. Marilyn Strathern, '"Improving ratings": audit in the British university system', p. 315

## The Language of Learning

1. Liz Morrish, 'A Feminist's Response to the Technologization of Discourse in British Universities', *European Journal of Women's Studies*, Vol. 7, No. 2, 2000, pp. 229–38
2. George Orwell, *Homage to Catalonia* (Harmondsworth, Penguin, 1962)
3. George Orwell, *1984*, (London, Penguin, 1989) and *Animal Farm* (London, Secker and Warburg, 1945)
4. George Orwell, *1984*, p. 213
5. See the discussion of the 1944 Education Act in David Morgan and Mary Evans, *The Battle for Britain: Citizenship and Ideology in the Second World War* (London, Routledge, 1993), pp. 128–31
6. Melanie Phillips, *All Must Have Prizes* (London, Time Warner Books, 1997)
7. See *The Future of Higher Education*, Cmnd. 5735 (London, DfES, 2003), p. 64
8. 'Trial by ordeal', *Guardian Education*, 30 January 2001, pp. 12–13
9. *The Future of Higher Education*, pp. 58–9
10. See the discussion of gender difference in D. L.

Rhode, *Speaking of Sex: The Denial of Gender Inequality* (Cambridge MA, Harvard University Press, 1997)

11. George Ritzer, *The McDonaldization Thesis* (London, Sage, 1998)

12. Mike Brake, 'I may be a Queer, but at least I am a Man: Male Hegemony and ascribed versus achieved gender', in D. L. Barker and S. Allen (eds), *Sexual Divisions and Society: Process and Change* (London, Tavistock, 1976)

## Gendered Spaces

1. Virginia Woolf, *Three Guineas* (Oxford, Oxford University Press, 1992)

2. *Three Guineas*, p. 309

3. *Three Guineas*, p. 242

4. Amartya Sen, *Development as Freedom* (Oxford, Oxford University Press, 2001)

5. Barbara Ehrenreich *et al.*, *Global Women: Nannies, Maids and Sex Workers in the New Economy* (London, Granta, 2003)

6. Jarrett Report, *Report of the Steering Committee for Efficiency Studies in Universities*

7. Linda Ray Pratt, 'Going Public: Political Discourse and the Faculty Voice', in M. Berube and C. Nelson (eds.), *Higher Education Under Fire* (New York, Routledge, 1995)

8. See the comments by Liz Morrish 'A Feminist's Response to the Technologization of Discourse in British Universities', p. 232

9. Norman Fairclough, *Critical Discourse Analysis* (Harlow, Longman, 1995)

10. Virginia Woolf, *A Room of One's Own* (Oxford, Oxford University Press, 1992), p. 22
11. Women's Studies Network Association (UK) Newsletter, No. 43, August 2003, pp. 16–17
12. Linda McDowell, *Capital Culture* (Oxford, Blackwell, 1997)
13. *Three Guineas*, p. 360
14. Richard Hoggart, *Between Two Worlds: Essays* (London, Arum Press, 2001), p. 195
15. Laura Flanders, *Bushwomen: Tales of a Cynical Species* (London, Verso, 2004)
16. Barbara Ehrenreich *et al.*, *Global Women: Nannies, Maids and Sex Workers in the New Economy*; Jan Jindy Pettman, *Worlding Women: A Feminist International Politics* (London, Routledge, 1996)
17. Mike Savage and Anne Witz (eds), *Gender and Bureaucracy* (Oxford, Blackwell, 1992)
18. M. L. Davies, 'University culture or intellectual culture?', in B. Brecher, O. Fleischmann and J. Halliday (eds), *The University in a Liberal State* (Aldershot, Avebury, 1996), p. 23
19. Elizabeth Bird, 'The Academic Arm of the Women's Liberation Movement', *Women's Studies International Forum*, Vol. 25, No. 1, 2002, pp. 139–49
20. *Three Guineas*, p. 360

## Iron Cages

1. Duke Maskell and Ian Robinson, *The New Idea of a University* (London, Haven, 2001)

2. George Ritzer, *The McDonaldization Thesis* (London, Sage, 1998)
3. David Harvey, *The Condition of Postmodernity* (Oxford, Blackwell, 1990); John Jervis, *Exploring the Modern* (Oxford, Blackwell, 1998); Jean-François Lyotard, *The Postmodern Condition* (Manchester, Manchester University Press, 1984); Marshall Berman, *All That Is Solid Melts Into Air* (London, Verso, 1982)
4. John Jervis, *Exploring the Modern*, p. 335
5. Raymond Williams, *The Long Revolution* (Harmondsworth, Penguin, 1965); Richard Hoggart, *The Uses of Literacy* (Harmondsworth, Penguin, 1958); E. P. Thompson, *The Making of the English Working Class* (London, Gollancz, 1963)
6. For example, Sheila Rowbotham, *Hidden from History* (London, Pluto, 1971); Monique Wittig, *The Straight Mind and Other Essays* (Boston, Beacon Press, 1992); Edward Said, *Culture and Imperialism* (London, Vintage, 1994)
7. Steven Shapin, 'Ivory Trade', *London Review of Books*, Vol. 25, No. 17, 11 September 2003, p. 19
8. Steven Shapin, 'Ivory Trade', p. 17
9. Robert D. Putnam, *Bowling Alone* (New York, Simon and Schuster, 2000), p. 413
10. Robert D. Putnam, *Bowling Alone*, p. 306
11. Michel Foucault, *Discipline and Punish* (London, Penguin, 1977)
12. Jane Austen, *Emma* (London, Everyman's Library, 1993), p. 19
13. Sylvia Plath, 'Daddy', in *Ariel* (London, Faber and Faber, 1965), pp. 54–5

14. Jacqueline Rose, *The Haunting of Sylvia Plath*, London, Virago, 1992)
15. Aurelia Schober Plath (ed.), *Letters Home: Correspondence 1950–1963* (New York, Harper and Row, 1975), p. 13
16. Ted Hughes, 'The Blue Flannel Suit', in *Birthday Letters* (London, Faber and Faber, 1998), p. 67

## Survival Strategies

1. Terry Eagleton, *The Gatekeeper: A Memoir* (London, Allen Lane, 2001) p. 141
2. See John Campbell, *Margaret Thatcher: Volume One, The Grocer's Daughter* (London, Jonathan Cape, 2000); Hilary Rose, *Love, Power and Knowledge* (London, Polity, 1994), pp. 150–3
3. David Lodge, *Changing Places* (Harmondsworth, Penguin, 1978)
4. Office of Science and Technology 'The Sustainability of University Research: A Consultation on Reforming Parts of the Dual Support System', (www.ost.gov.uk/policy/universityresearch.pdf)
5. '2001 Research Assessment Exercise: The Outcome', (http://www.hero.ac.uk/rae/Pubs/4_01/section1.htm)
6. Virginia Woolf, *Three Guineas*, p. 193
7. A. H. Halsey, H. Lauder, P. Brown and A. Stuart Wells (eds) *Education: Culture, Economy, Society* (Oxford, Oxford University Press, 1997); Pierre Bourdieu, *Distinction: A Social*

*Critique of the Judgement of Taste* (London, Routledge, 1986)

8. Beverley Skeggs, *Formations of Class and Gender* (London, Sage, 1997); Linda McDowell, *Capital Cultures* (Oxford, Blackwell, 1997)

9. Pierre Bourdieu, 'The Economy of Symbolic Goods', in *Practical Reason*, p. 106

# Index